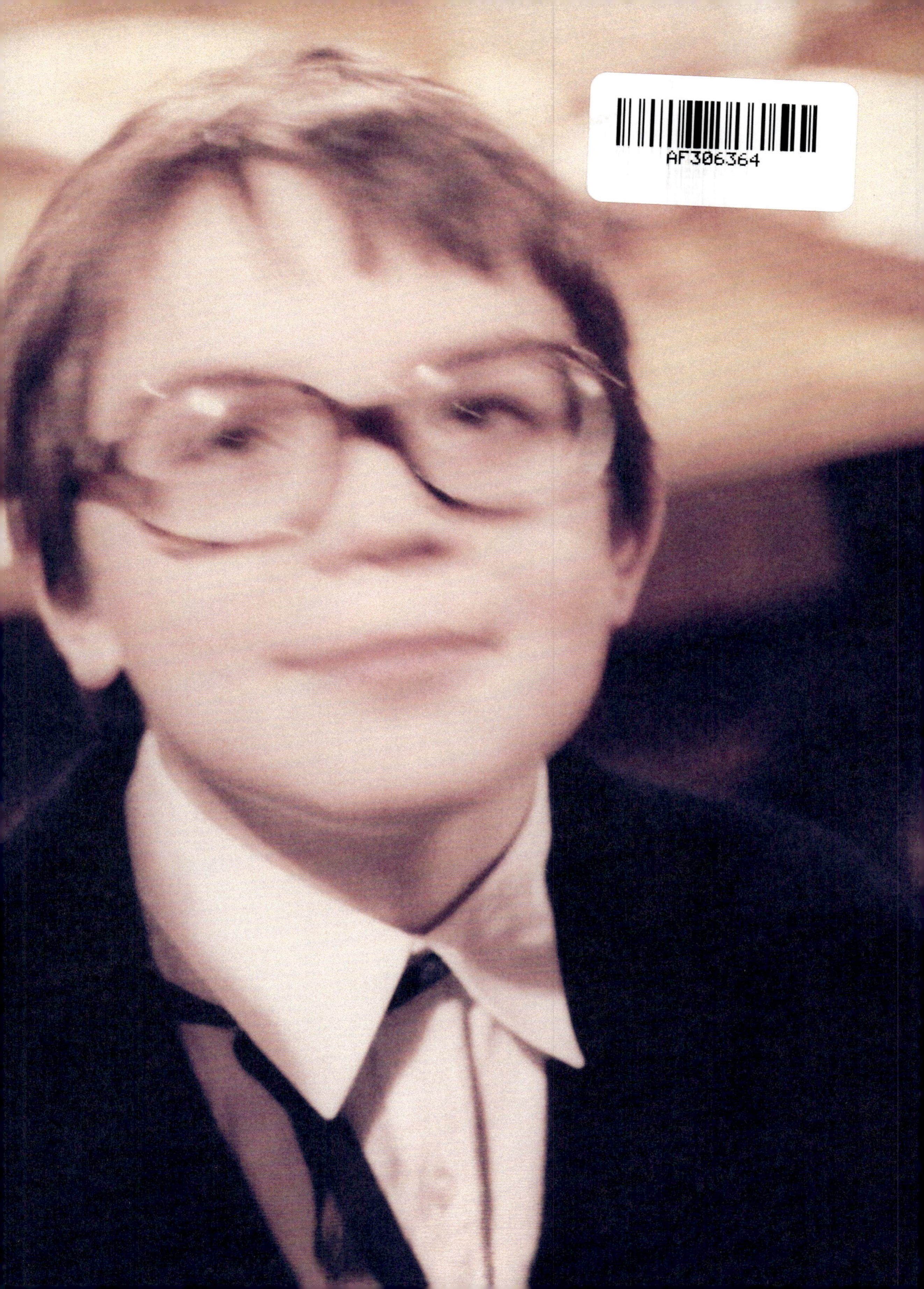
AF306364

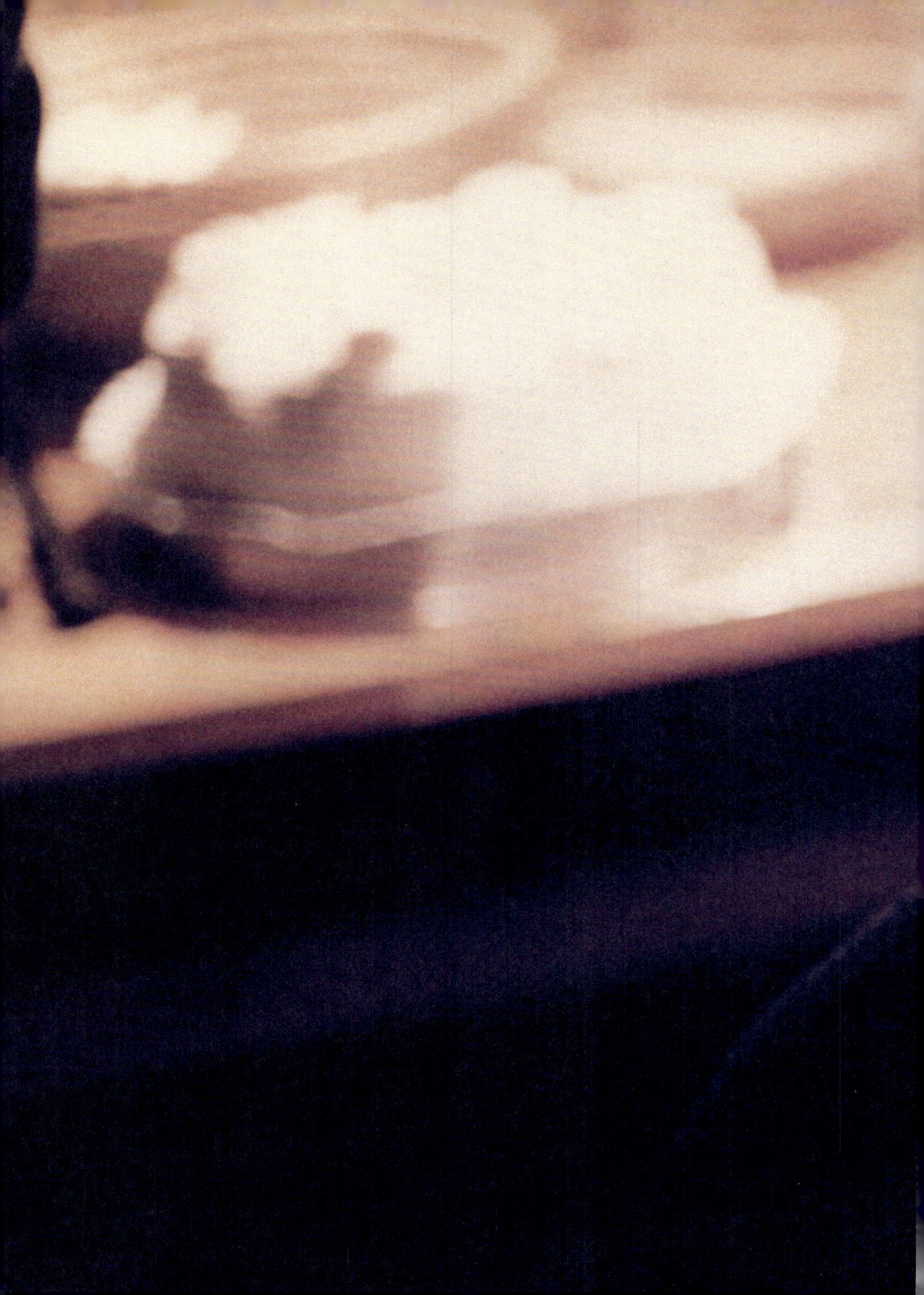

The childhood of my memory was an unwelcoming world, a world in which I existed but was not seen.

With a text by Sonja Busch, founder of the European Association for Holotropic Breathwork, and an epilogue by Manfred Nowak, United Nations Independent Expert for the UN Global Study on Children Deprived of Liberty

Verlag für moderne Kunst

The childhood of my memory is a story of transformation
and healing; a very personal journey to my heart
and to a self, worthy of love and life.

This book provides insight into an autobiographical analysis
of traumatic experiences of childhood abuse. Only decades
afterwards was I able to process the painful memories of
my own experiences, alongside growing signs of depression
and isolation. Regular, intensive therapy sessions became
part of my everyday existence and I found I could express
my memories in paintings, drawings, text and photography
in order to give a name and form to the unspeakable.

I can't imagine that there could be a more personal, more
intimate book. Through these means, I have come to identify
with my own life story and to share myself with the world.

My biography is not an isolated case. Shame, as their lone
companion, separates victims from a good and self determined
life, even after years of suffering. I hope that the following
pages will shed light on the extent of the suffering that
can result from abuse in our society, and in particular from
ritual abuse, and that the collective silence can be
transformed into an open dialogue.

I would like to whole-heartedly thank Sonja Busch and
Thomas Liska for having stood by me in my most difficult
moments and for their very humane personal and
therapeutic support. It became clear to me that healing
is possible, that it can happen.

My special thanks also go to the designer Clemens Schedler
for his soulful and trusted collaboration on this publication.
Friends have accompanied me throughout the years
and accepted me without reservation. For this I give my
sincere thanks.

Laurent Ziegler

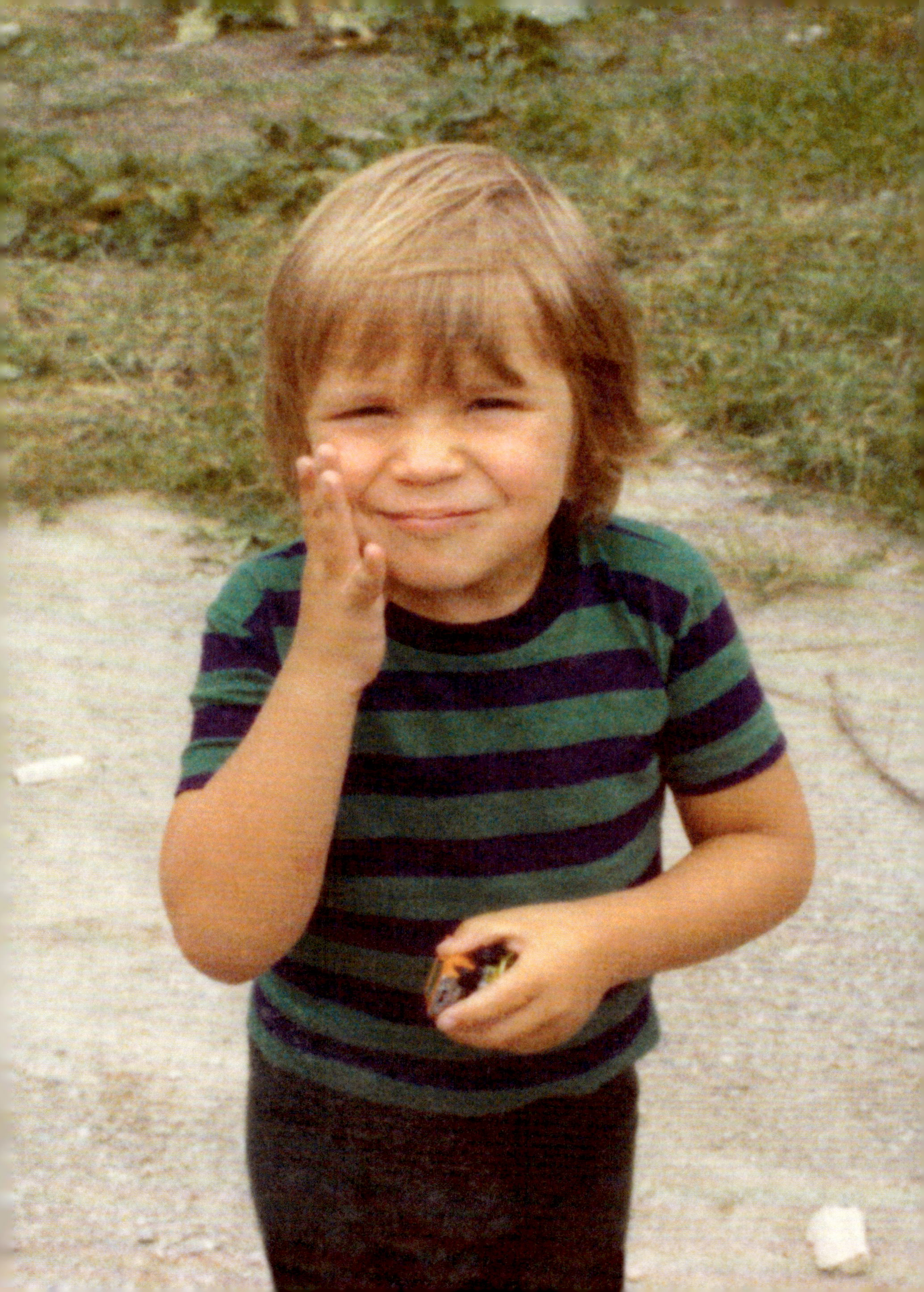

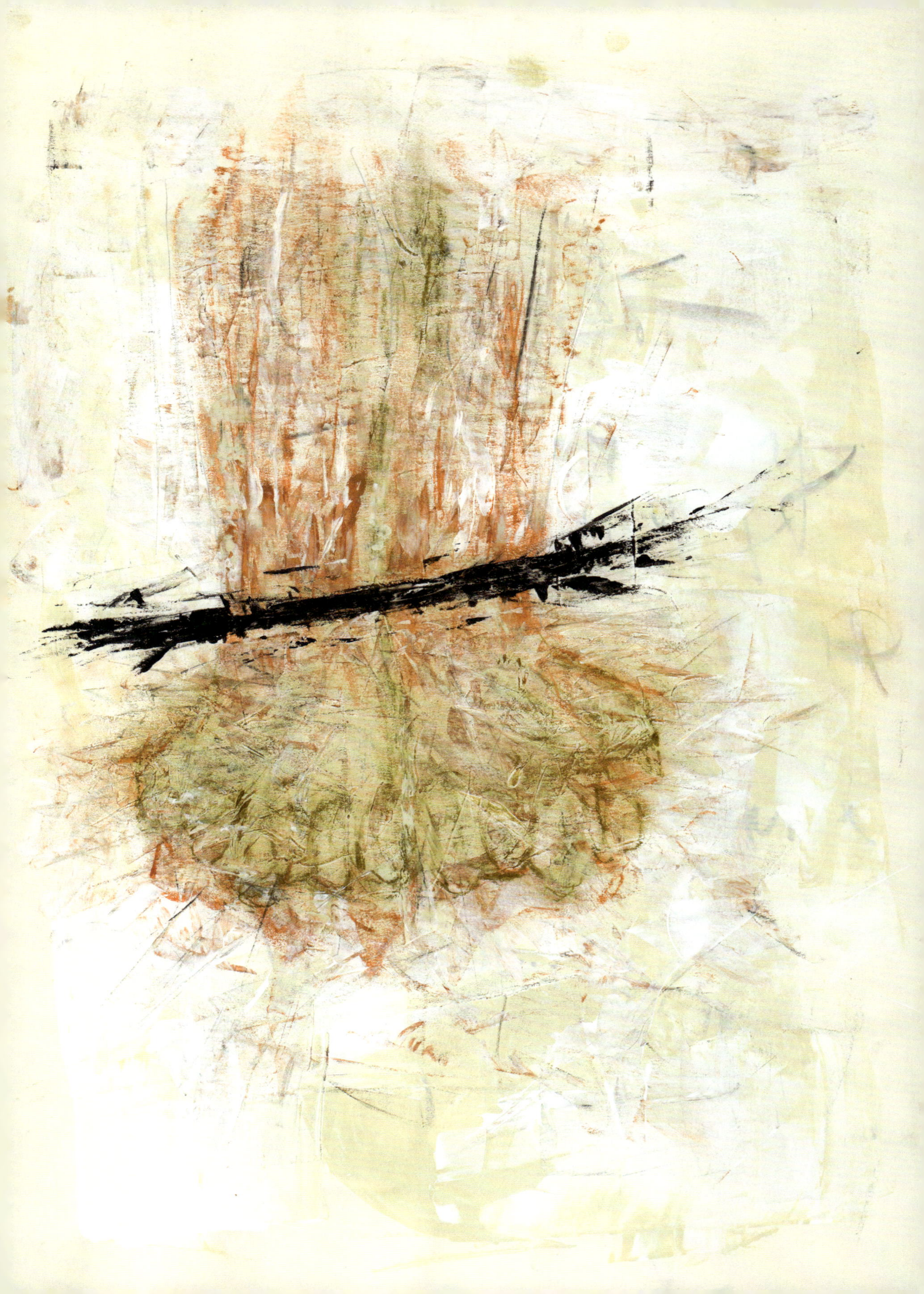

There are hardly any pictures
for I was hardly "there."
I remember my shoes, too tight,
the men and my mother's beatings,
the shared bedroom,
the rolled-up carpets of her parents,
a hiding place under the table
or behind the stove.

I see the fears in my life,
deprivation in my eyes,
a shadow within me.
And I want to live,
to step out of the darkness.
There's a long way to go.

I say to myself:
I am acceptable; reasonable,
worthy of being felt and heard,
loving, engaging, curious,
with the hope and desire
to create.

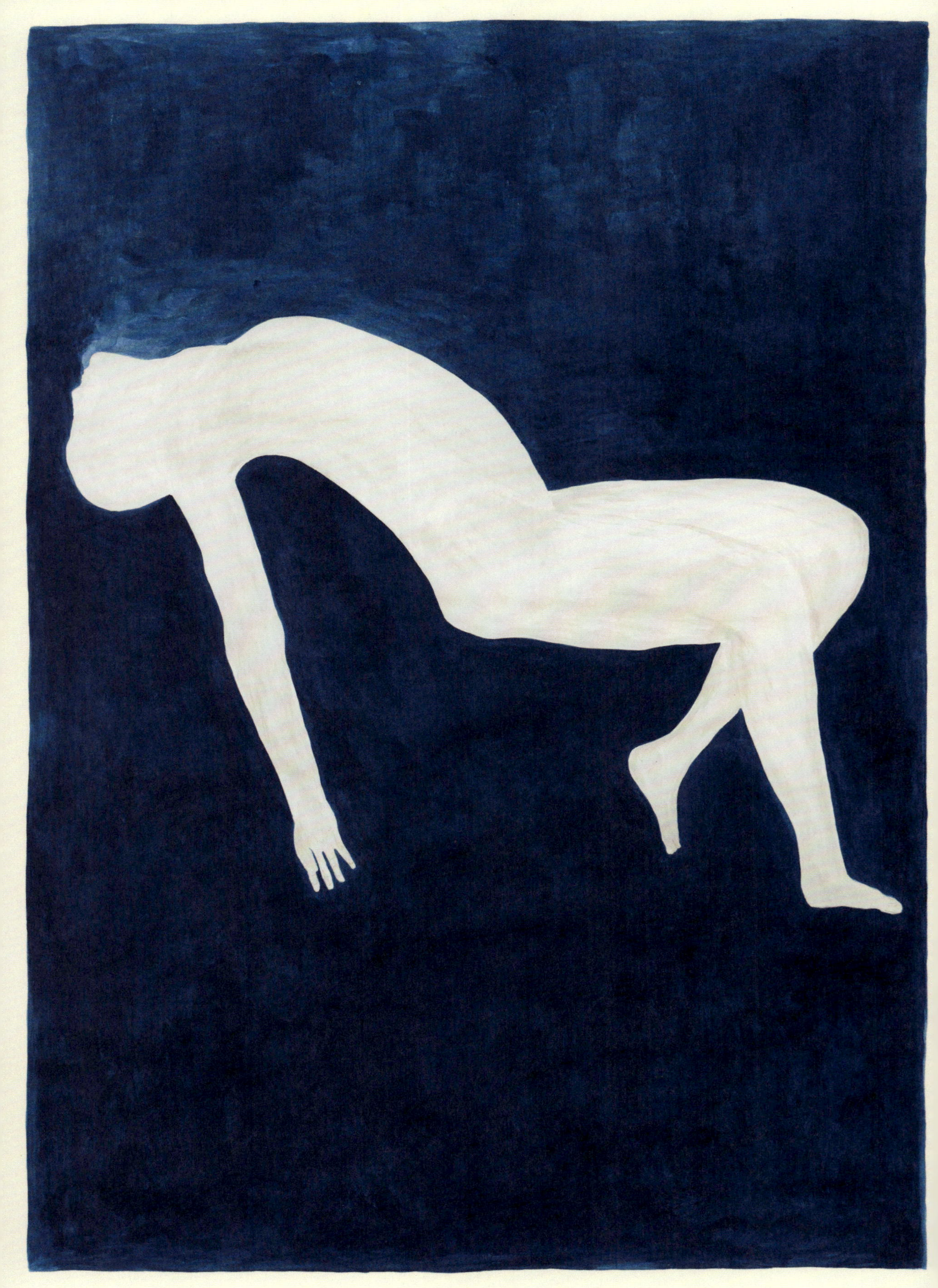

I am seeping out, seeping out of myself.
Don't want to heal, to convalesce.
A life after life;
where to place the shame?

Fingertips touch the fissure,
a deep crevice in my world,
forgiveness after the act,
the door closes.

A scream,
breathless, staring into a void,
foreboding is a delicate child,
an eye socket,
a mouth.

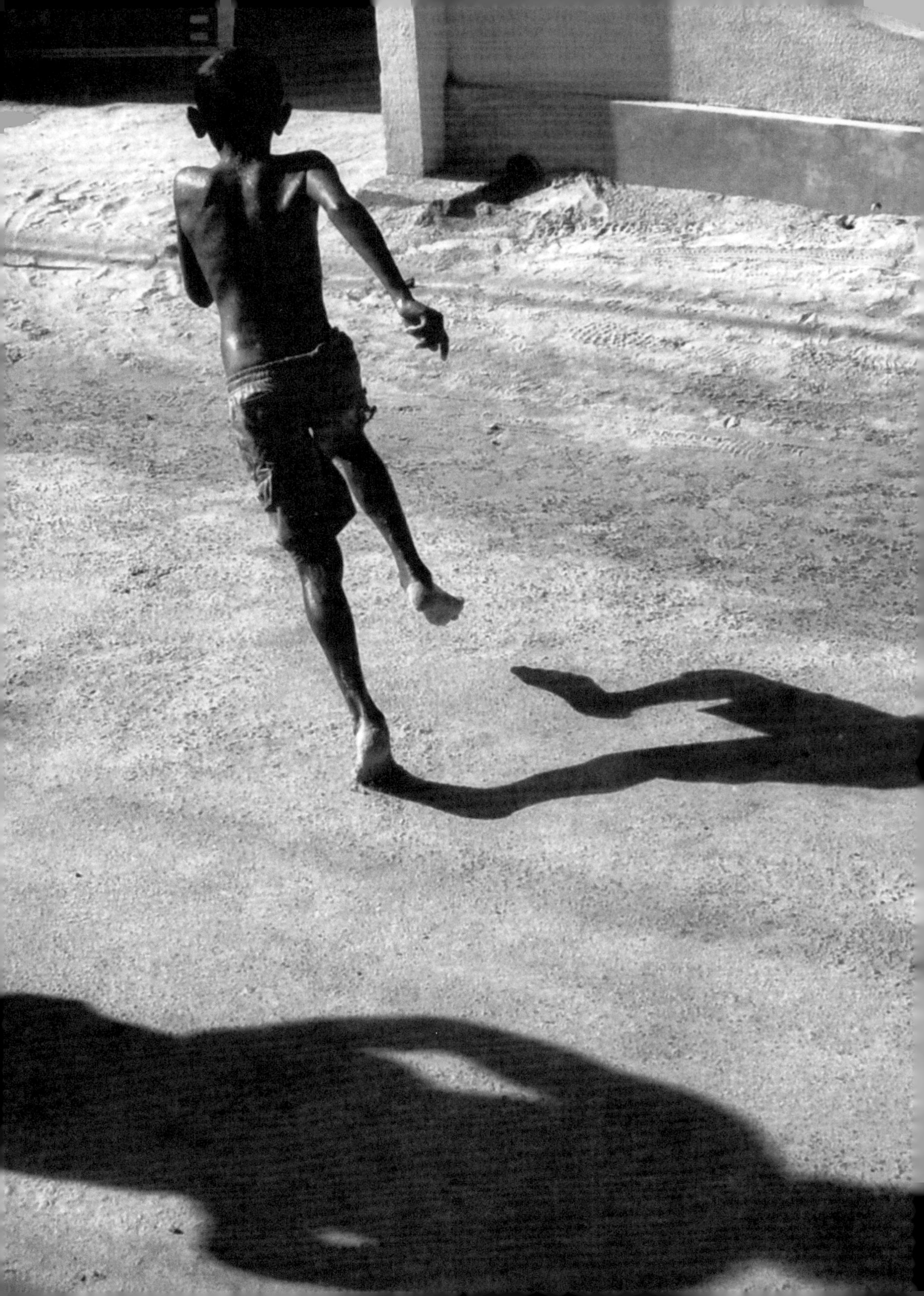

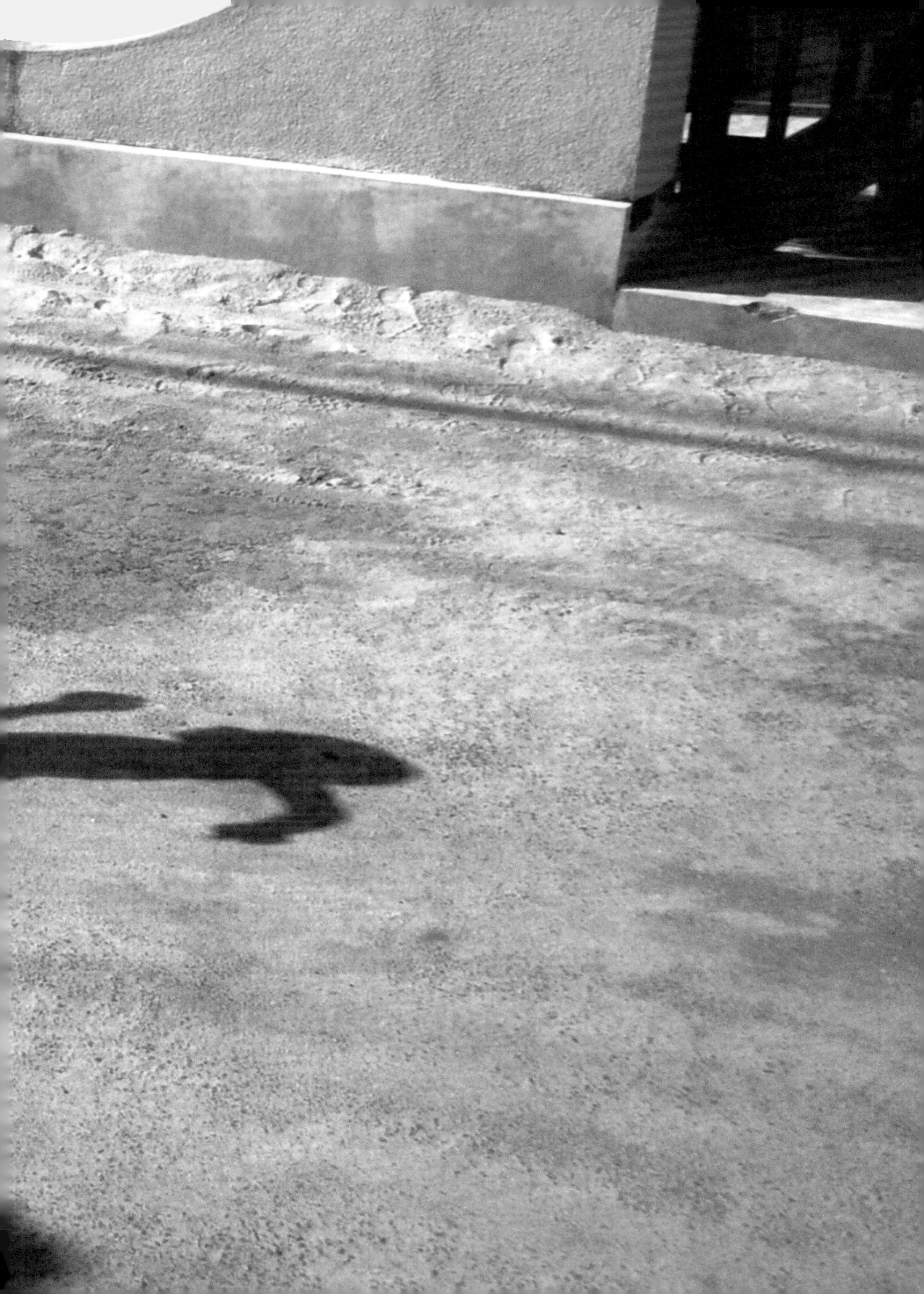

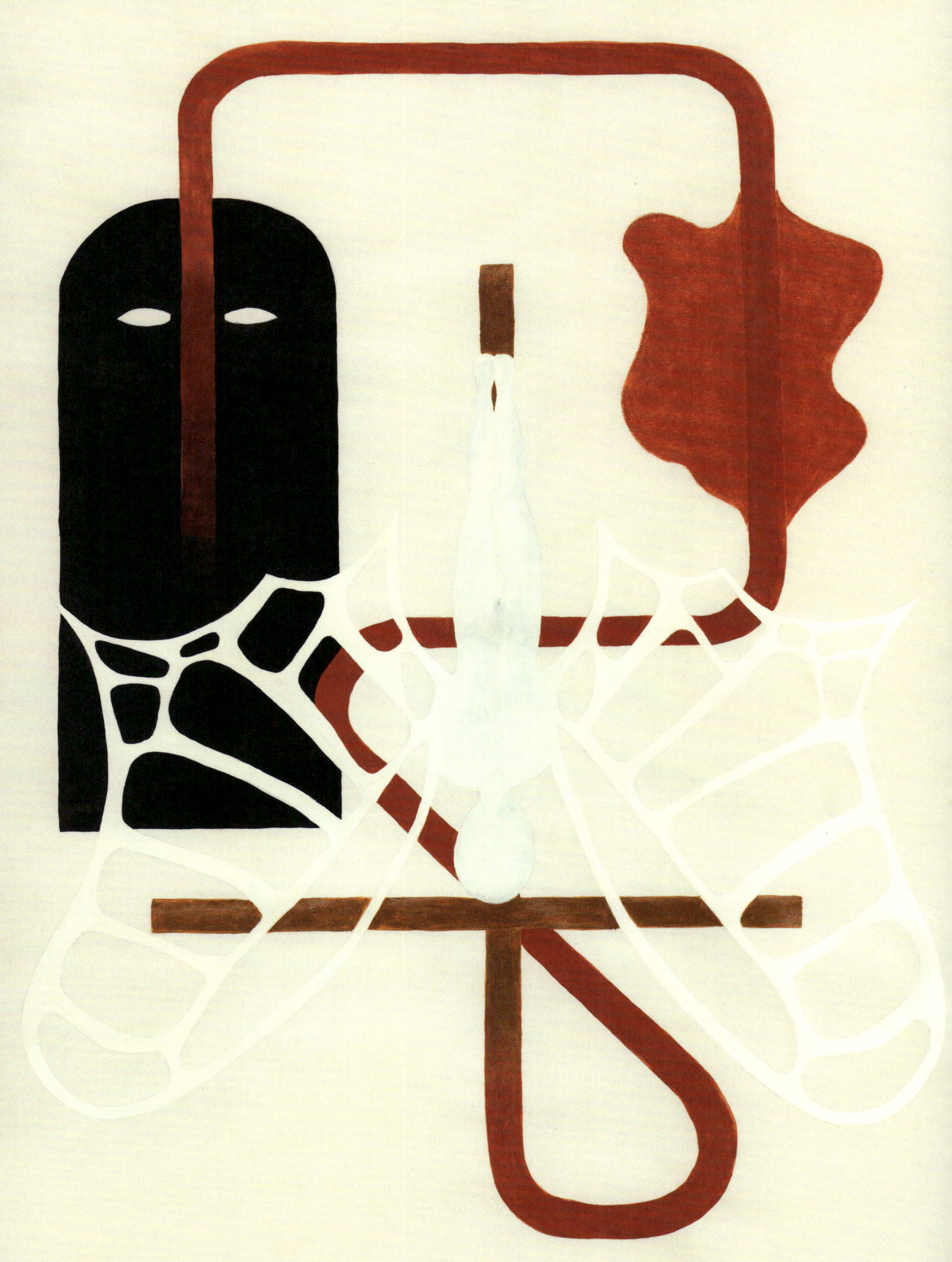

I was so young when
everything began.
The fear of not being
adequate shaped my
childhood. The yearn-
ing for tenderness
resulted in beatings.
Intimacy equaled
danger. Was I not able
to cope with my
mother's rejection?
Before which God
did I belittle myself?
My safe haven
was the gateway
to hell.

Small cars and airplanes
are my entry tickets
into a fantastic world.
My upper body plays
along and my arms
keep me on course.
My pelvis is attached
to the ground, sunken
into the ground
rigid, immobile,
and weak.

I live free, I am free.
I am my own person.
I am allowed to see,
to celebrate myself,
to be proud of and to
trust myself, to give
myself space and
importance.

Who was I before I was
hurt? Few keepsakes
remain. I held my breath
and tiptoed around.
Why did I run away
from home and where
did I go?

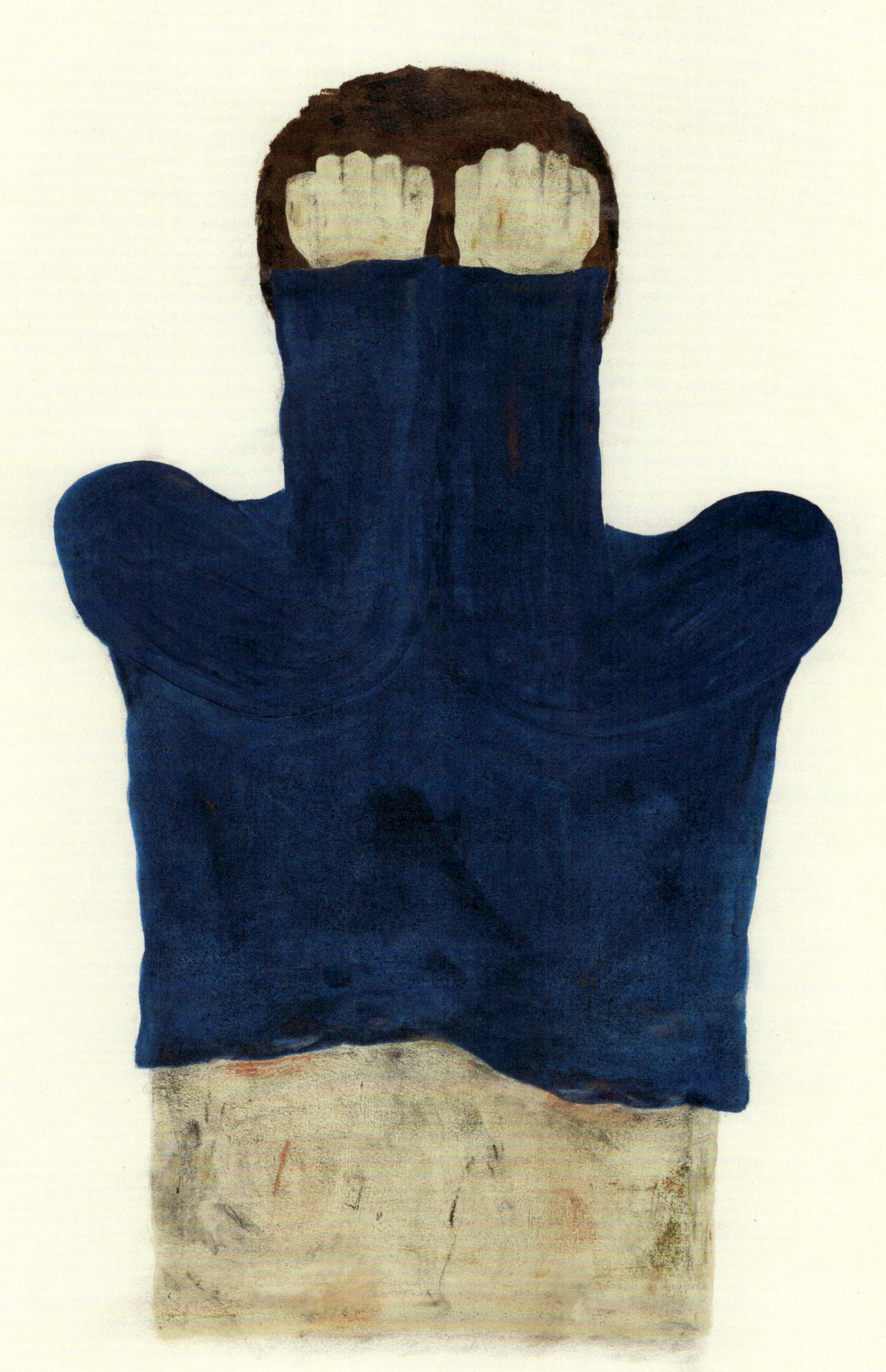

I am afraid.

I do not want to be **a victim and yet I feel powerless.** It seems to me that I never belonged to the here and now. I was molested as a child and ask myself: how was this possible?

My hands begin to shake, I hide my face, make myself small, and flail around for protection. I feel like I'm being handed over. I pound my head and gasp, strangled, for air. How long has it taken me to face my self-inflicted injuries? I would like to infuse all of my broken parts with trust and love.

Dreams accompany me throughout the day. Insects endure bloody torment until disfigured beyond recognition. A black hole is all that remains, its edges rimmed with pain like an eye that looks inward or a void with no reflection, an emptiness with no depth, a dried-out, flattened-out sea.

I think about my grandmother and about how she lived in fear. She told me that there are evil men out there. I should not have anything to do with them.

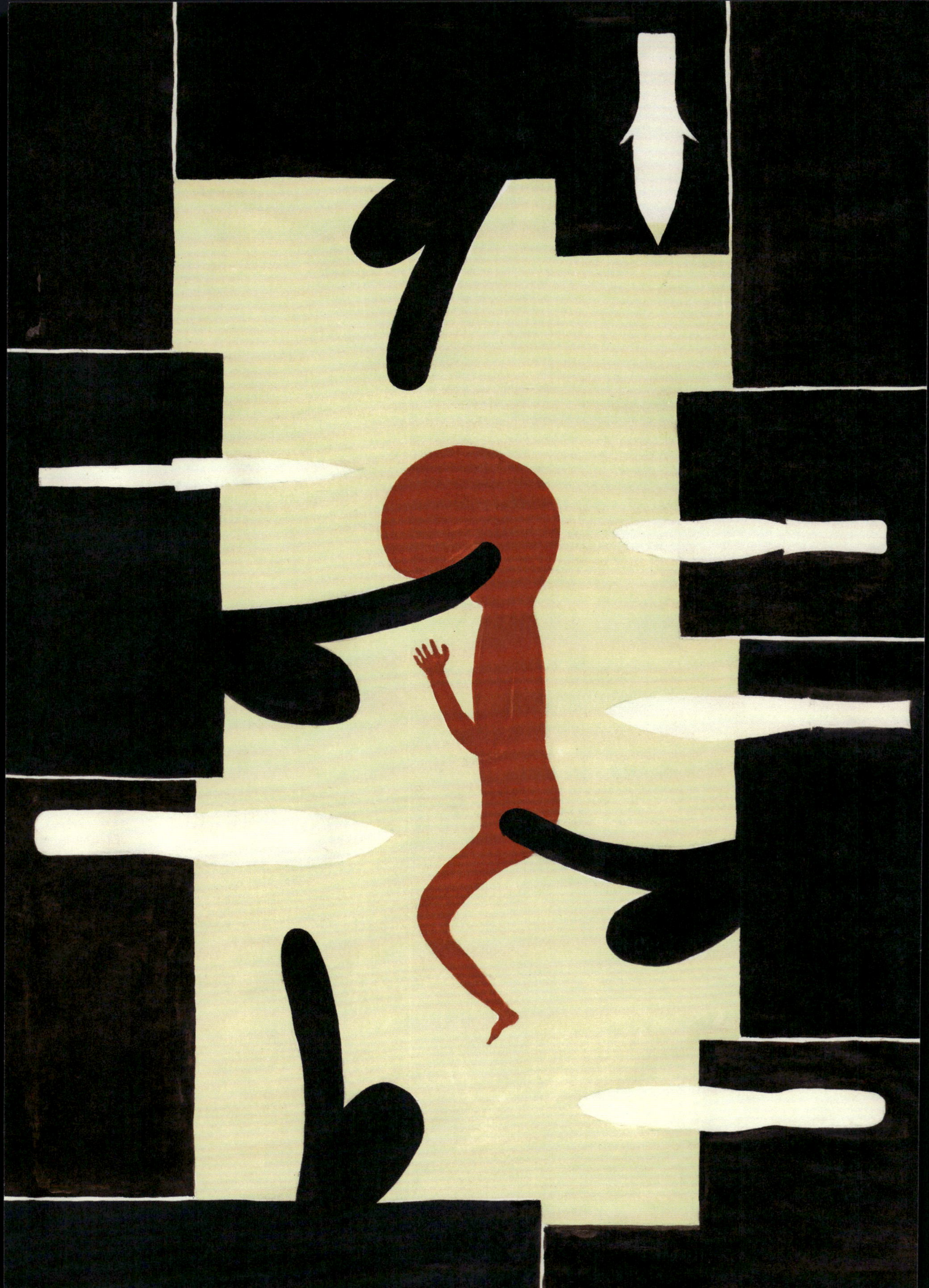

Sinking into unknown depths, my body breathes quietly. I see a dark room with curtains through which faint light passes. I feel the cold. There is a crib. I wrap my arms around myself, make myself small. Something foreign enters and penetrates me, hurts me deep inside. I don't want to be seen and struggle for air, to be free. There is too little air to breathe. Someone is squeezing my throat.

Once again, there is a dark room that appears empty and abandoned. I move towards a light on the other side and am thrown against a wall by hands, feet, and bodies that I can't exactly remember.

I am not alone, there are other children. My legs are twisted around so I can't run. I lie on my side on the floor, shield my pelvis and genitals. Now I am alone.

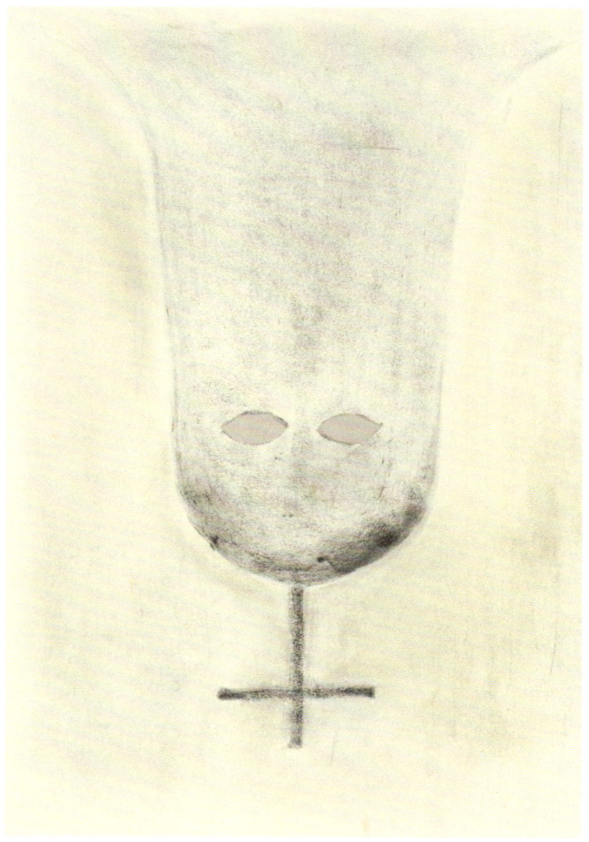

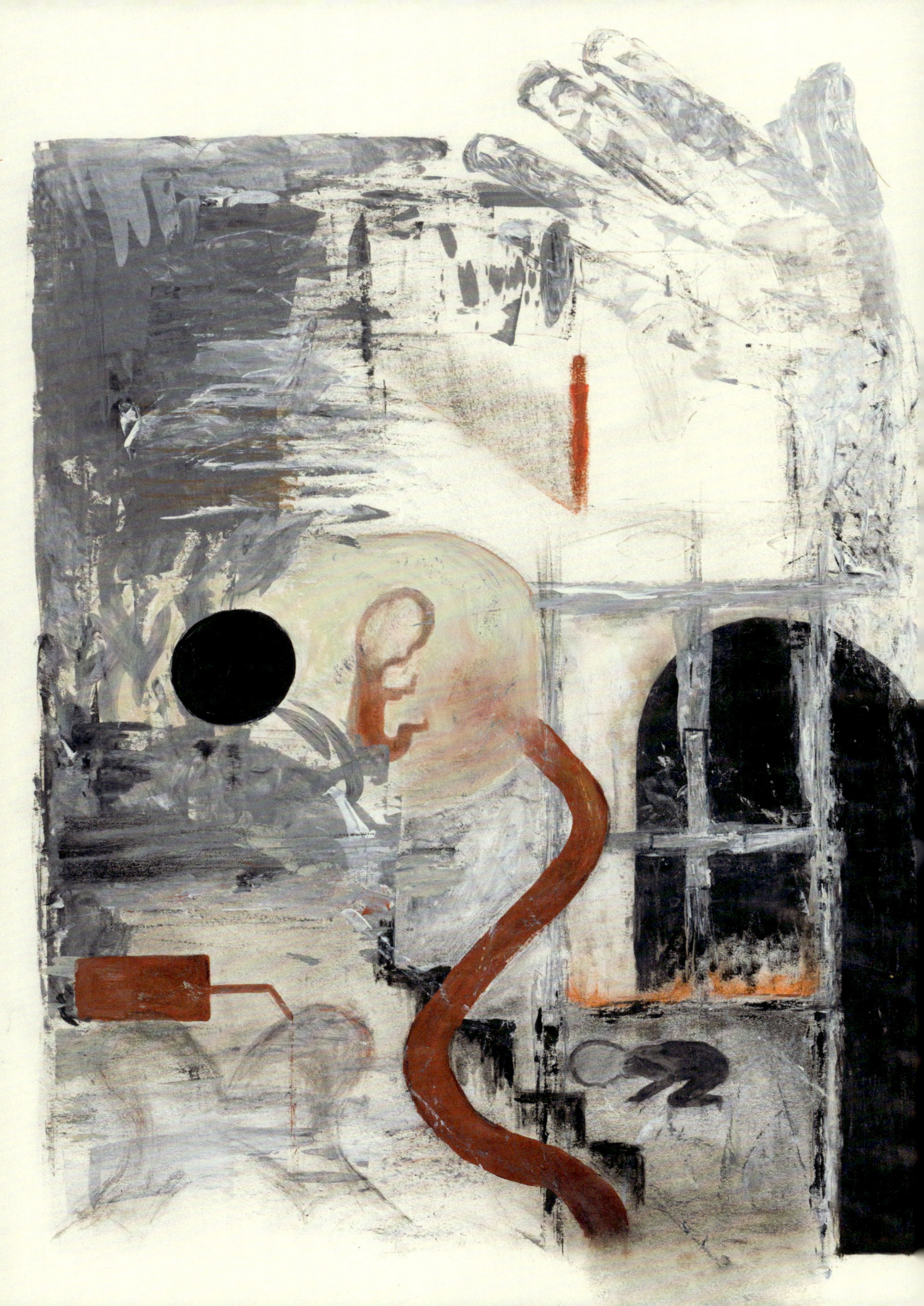

**Everything is bathed
in a dim light** behind
dull and dirty glass.
I am defenseless,
besieged by
enormous, dark
images, threatened
and smothered.

**I promised not to
forget the other
children.** I shoulder
their pain in order
to carry them back
into existence.
Can I ever leave
my past behind
and live?

**My shame
is re-examined.
My wounds won't
heal.** Sometimes
I found "being
possessed"
to be exciting,
pleasurable.

**Quiet are the paths
upon which my
dreams walk.** I am
confused. I so long
for healing.

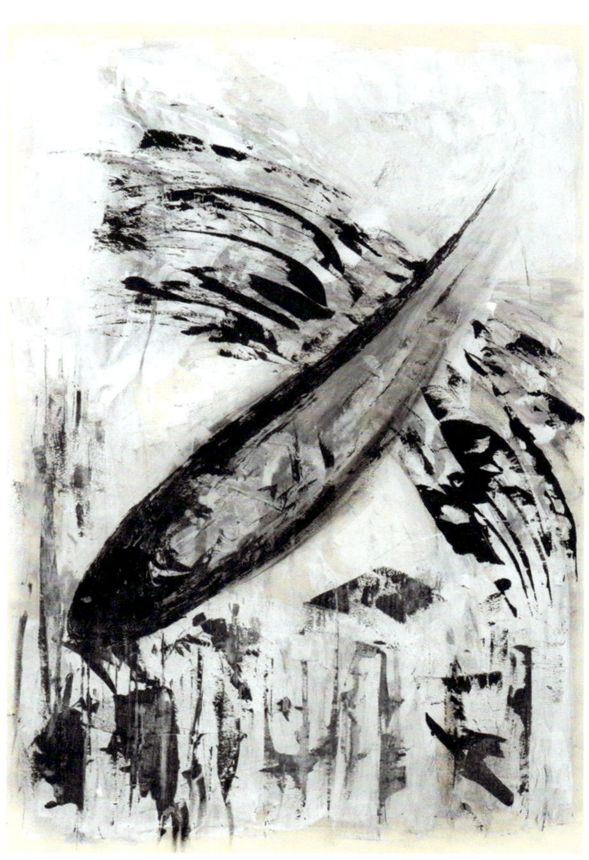

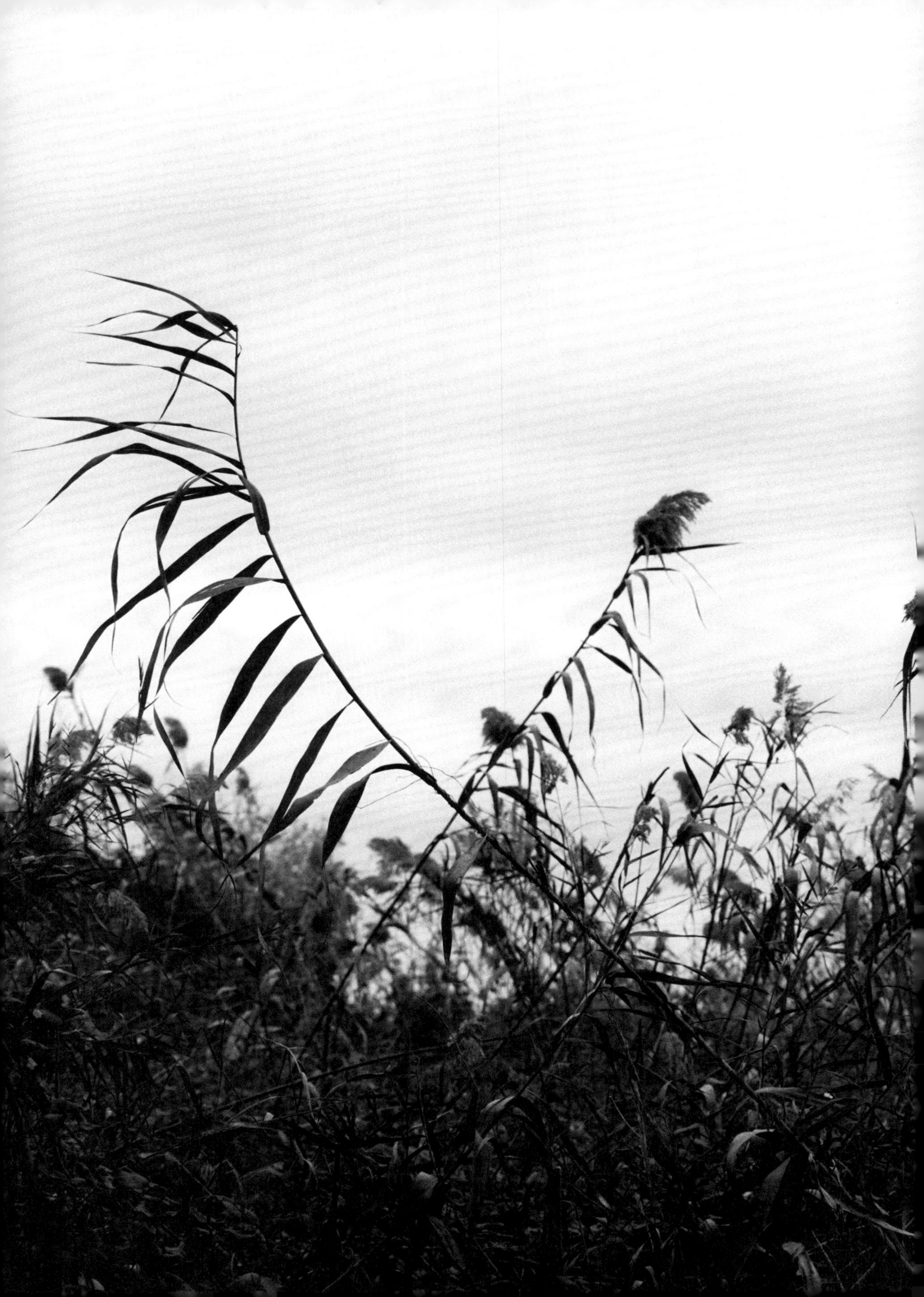

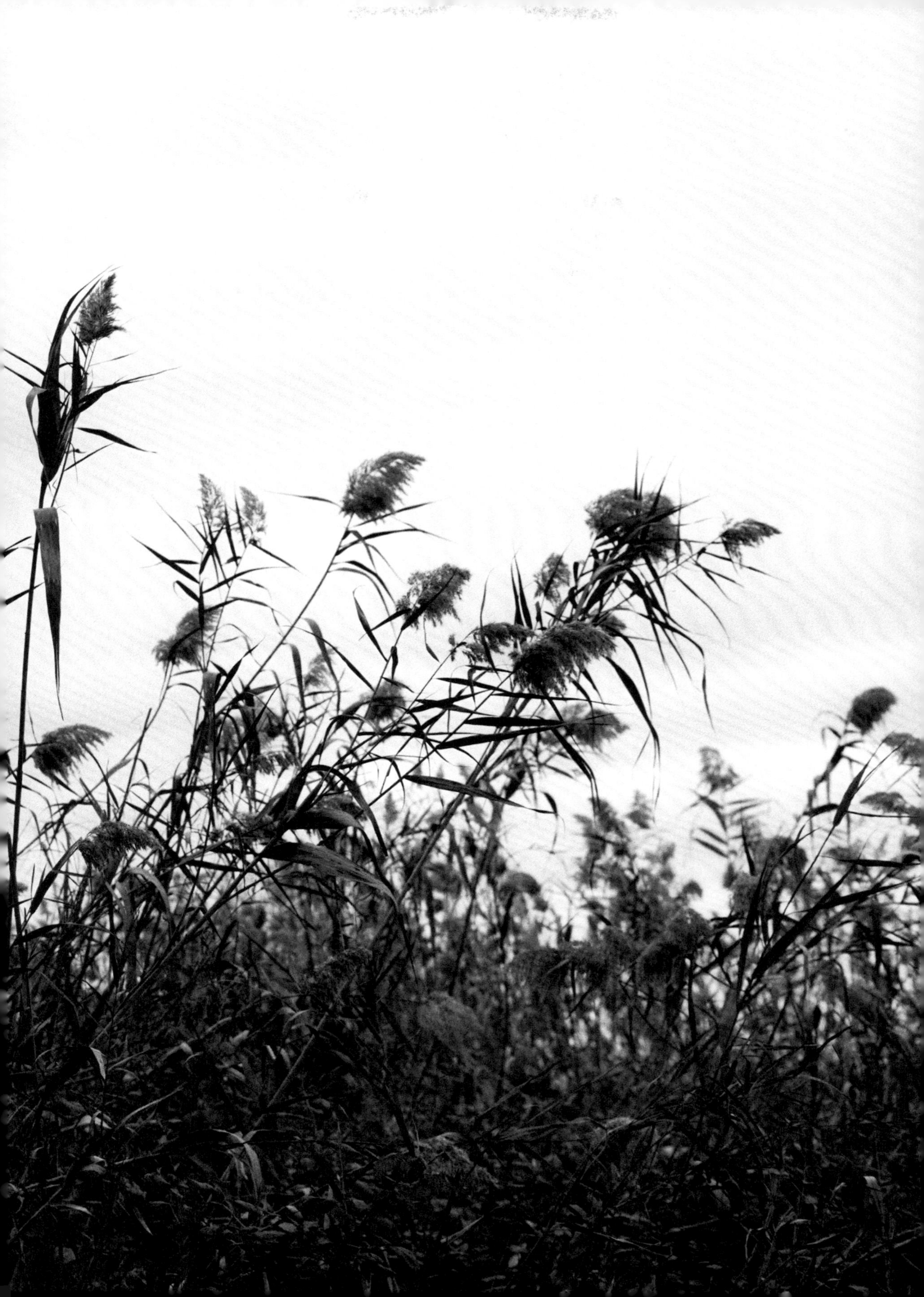

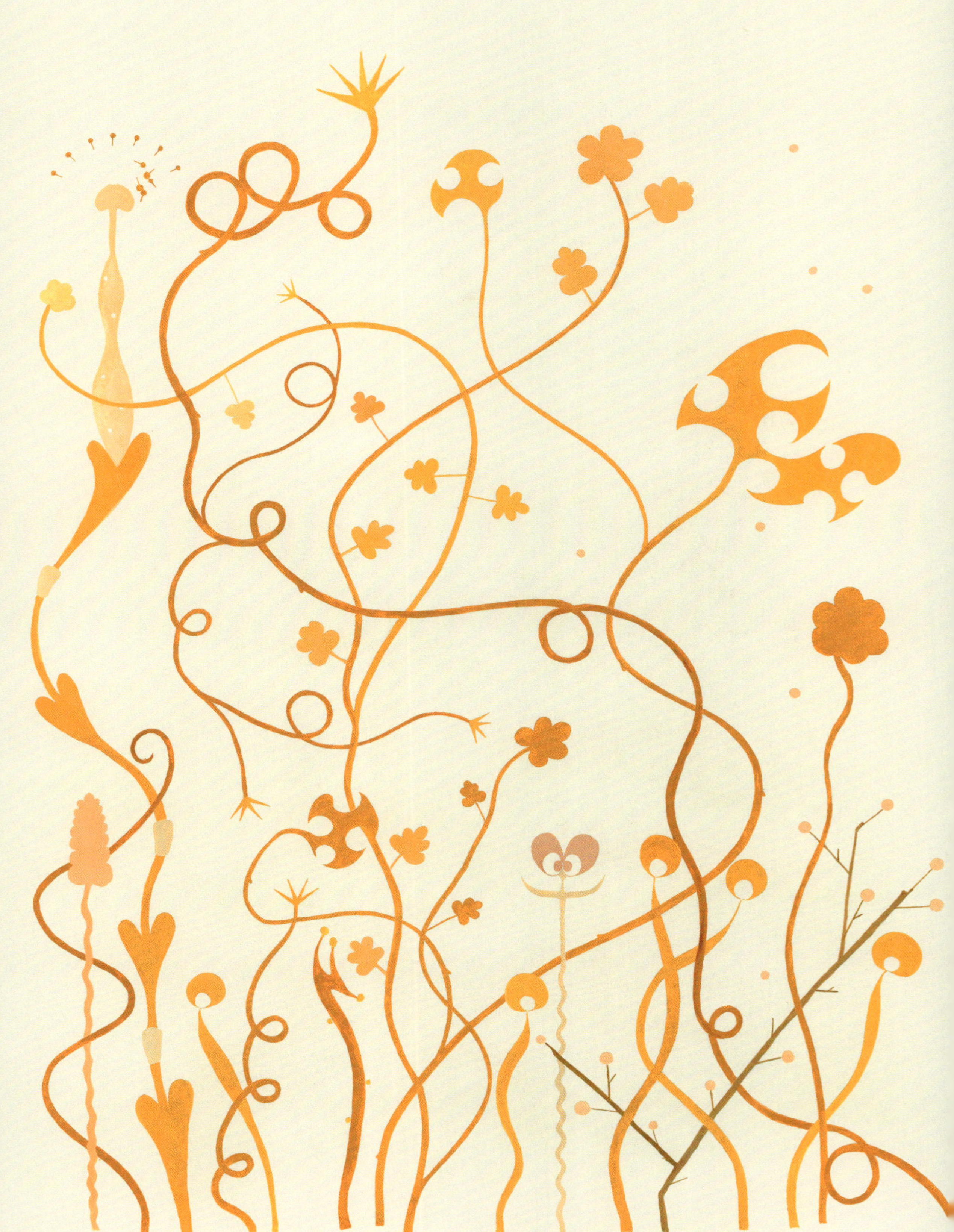

**I meander
along a path of dreams,
my soul inspired
by the love of many people.**

I break free,
begin to open my eyes,
to see, to breathe,
to hear the waves
beat against the walls.
I am ready.

**I often repeat my name —
Laurent, Laurent, Laurent …**

To remind myself
that I exist,
to reassure myself
that I am there
and was always there.

Laurent, I am with you.
You are not alone.
Nothing can harm you anymore.

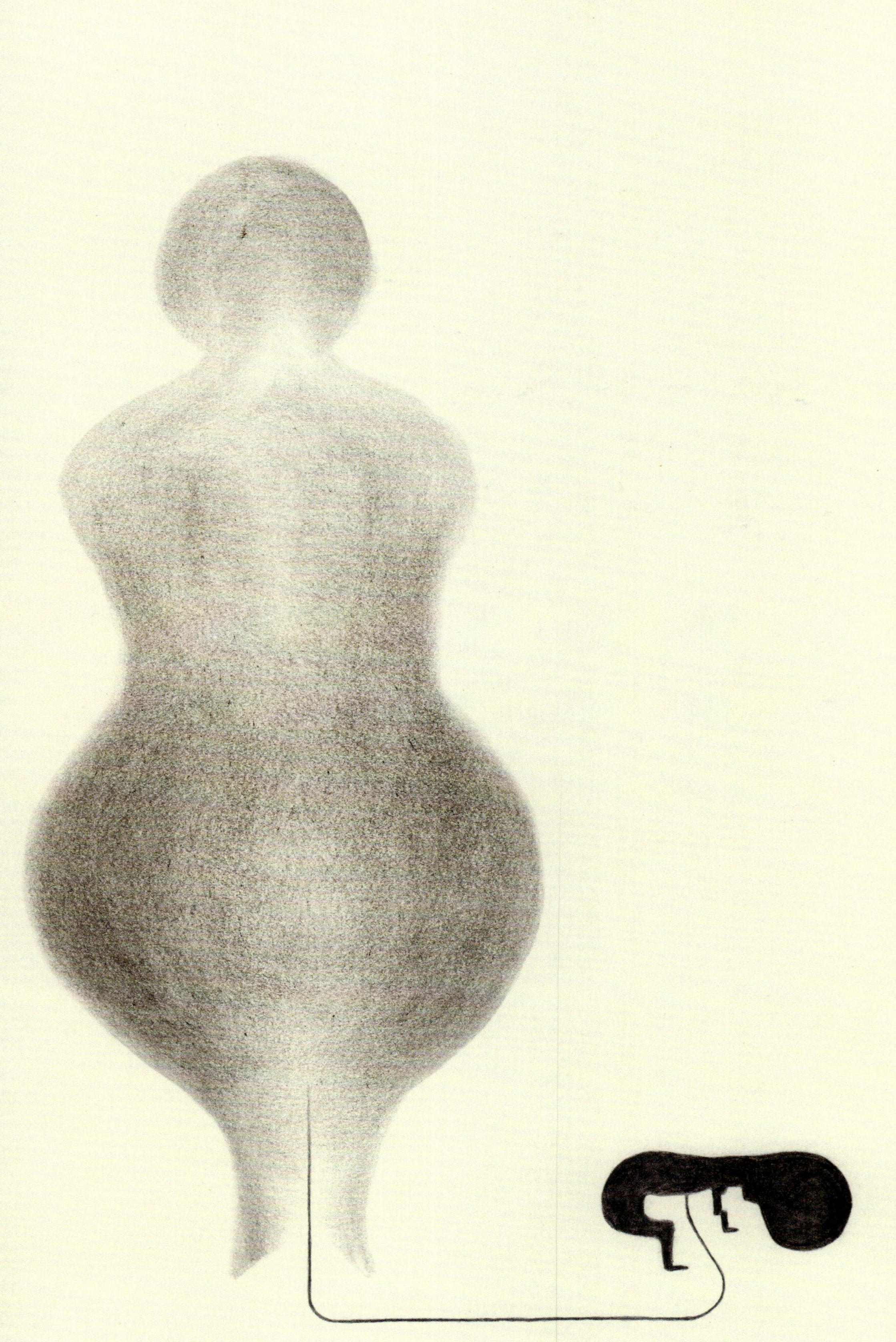

Gray clouds obscure the view. I feel lonely and disconnected from reality. I have been spirited off and locked away, left alone with my sadness and shame. It's clear that I will never be able to rise above this condition and dare to look other people in the eyes.

I have a dream about my mother and about how she is sent to a hospital. I don't want to go there. As the door opens, there is a smell of evil and death. I obey my heart and leave that place.

My inner child wants to participate in life and is therefore punished. I am traumatized by the way my parents "cared" for me: neglect, violence, isolation.

Life is a miracle. I feel the deepest gratitude, free myself from my helpless condition, and leave the pain behind.

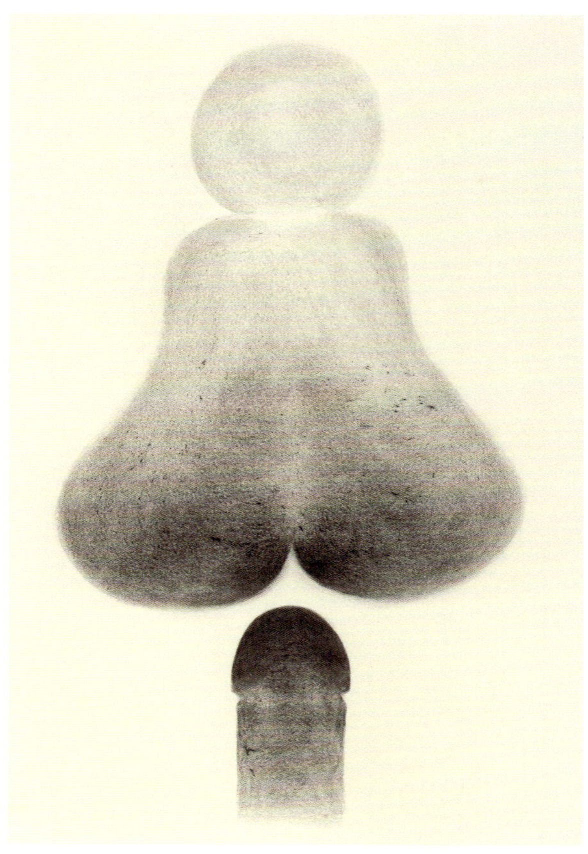

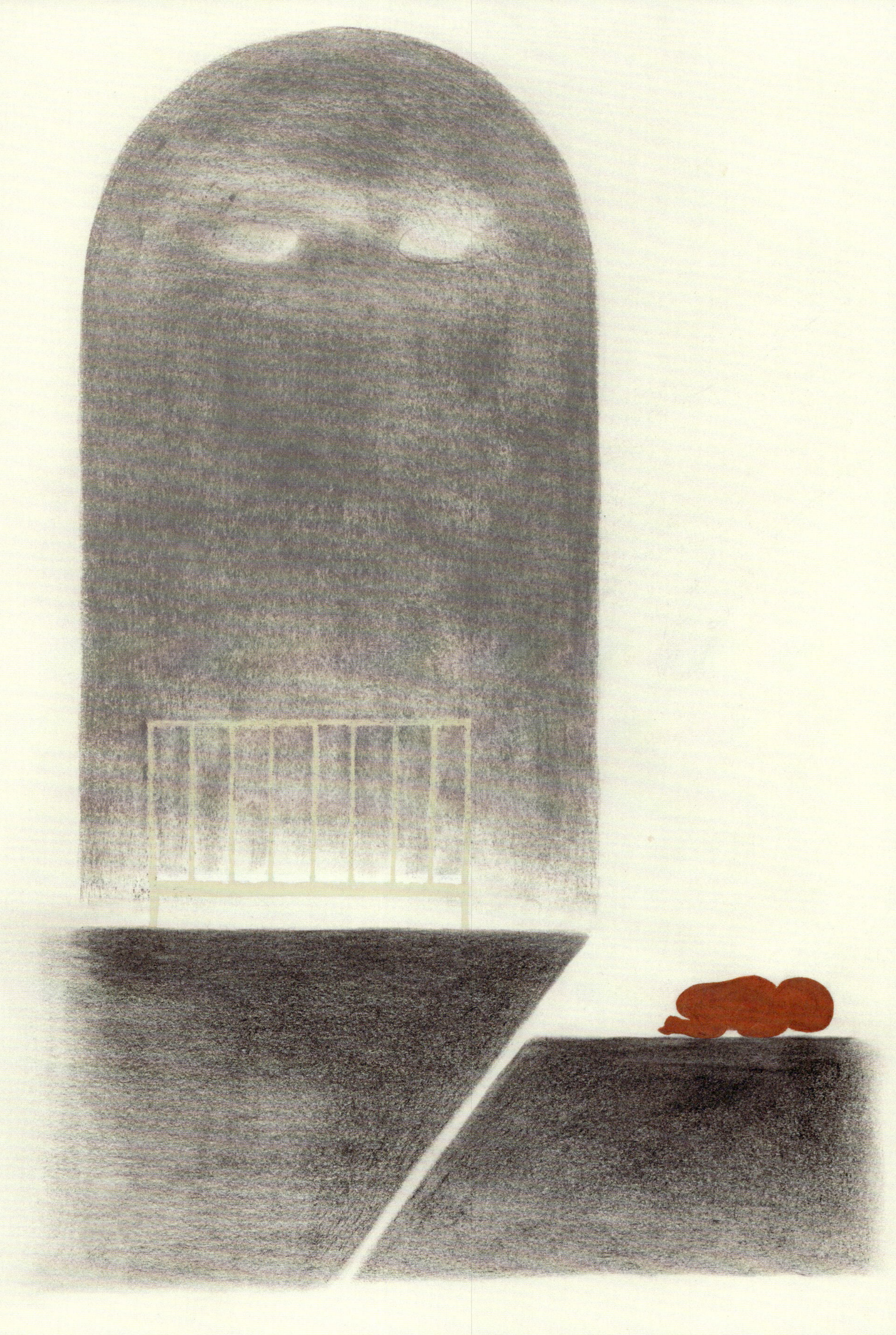

**My body timidly
entrusts me with the
memory of how I
was held, restrained,
beaten, penetrated.**
I see myself from above
in my childhood bed,
encircled by men.
Later, I am alone in
this bed, the room
is cold, my lower body
rigid. I see myself
from above, buried in
darkness.

**I crouch on my knees
in a dim room lit by
candles. Silence.** There
are hooded figures all
around. In the middle
lies a wooden cross
with narrow crosspieces
curved upwards.
A boy is placed on it,
naked and motionless,
with closed eyes.
I don't know if he is
still alive.

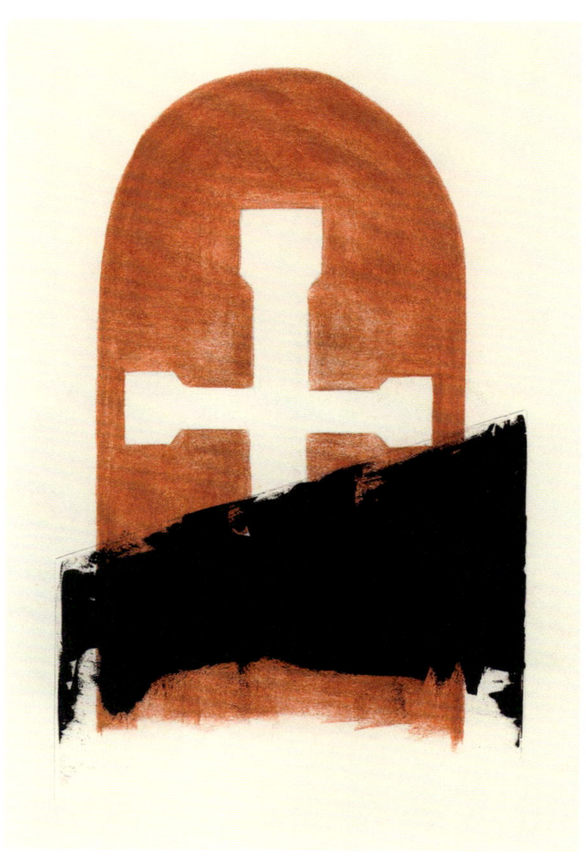

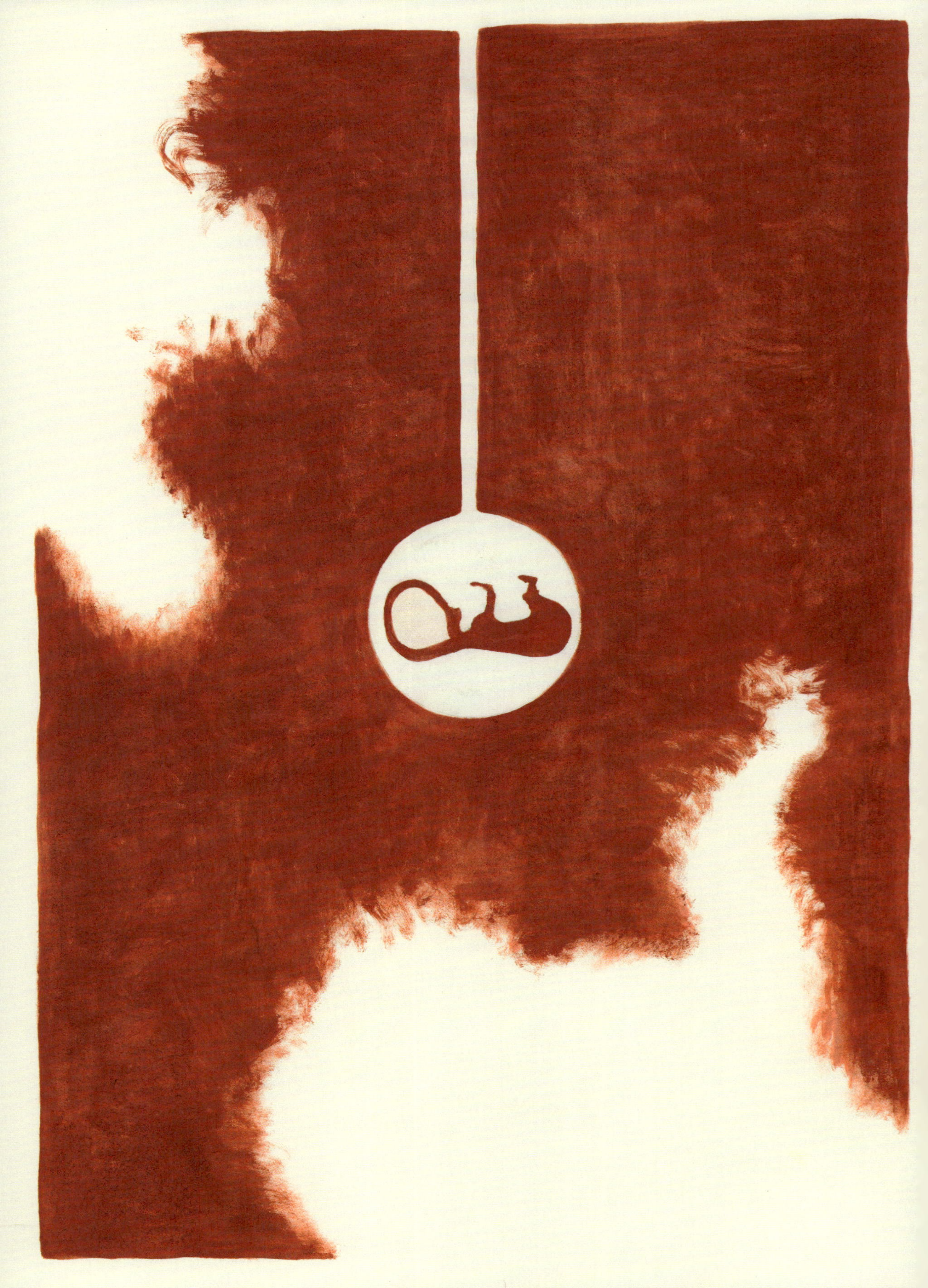

**The vessel of my body
has become one with
my memories and my
consciousness splits
away.** I am contorted,
breathless, constricted,
and in pain, restrained
by hands that I can't
see. I only know that
there are many of them
and there is no way
to break free.

**I try to protect myself
from being abused,**
pulling a cover over my
lower body. I am picked
up and laid over an
injured child, remember
open wounds and blood,
also death. There are
other children, several
of them, and I stroke
their arms. One child
is stretched out in
a vice, another hangs
from ropes. The latter
is very small and thin,
and dangles by his arms
and legs. There are
screams and a whimper.
Then silence. I have
a bond with them.
We serve as each others'
witnesses, in a way
that transcends death.

**My "so-called" perfect
childhood** — unwanted
attention, beatings
at school and an overly
sexualized behavior.
I was not clean, hid in
corners, had no friends.
I write about my life
and how I was shaped
by circumstances.
I believe in the right to
a self-determined life.

**The self-hatred is
becoming more
and more extreme.**
I want to injure
myself badly, beat
myself to death.
I loathe myself deeply
and take all the blame.
There's no place
left for love and
acceptance.

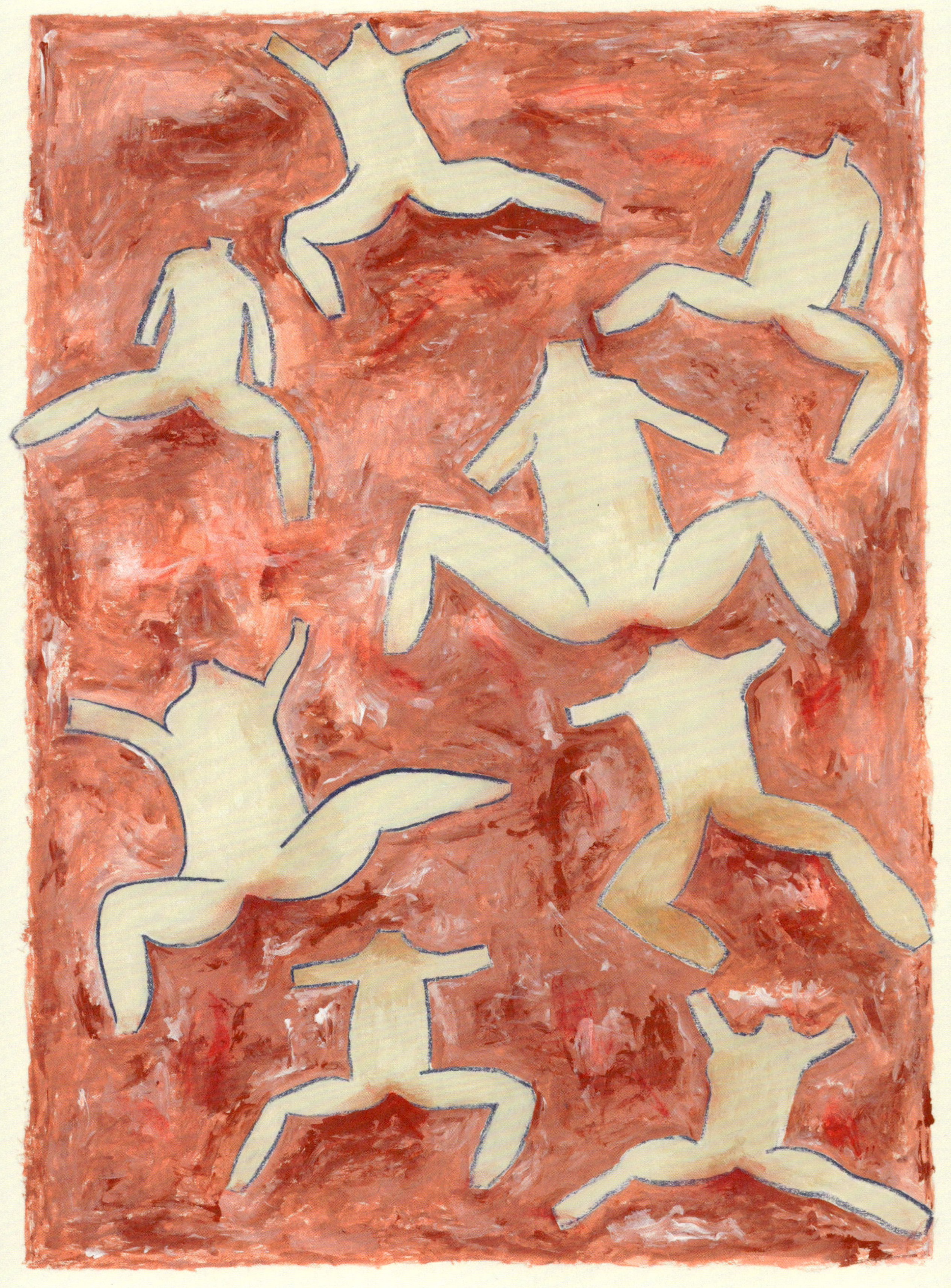

I am lying on a wooden cross, my feet bound, **my upper body moving freely.** Liquids are poured over me. I cannot recognize anyone, but I am not alone. My head feels like it has been injured. I make myself small and repeat my name — very softly, over and over.

Beatings mean that I have done something wrong, that I am guilty and am getting what I deserve. Deafness sets in.

My mind saved me when I was little. Now it's time to be grateful for the awareness and protection it gave me. Today I can make my way back to the heart, to relinquish control and surrender freely. My heart will support me on this journey and in all of the aftermath. My life is totally different now and that's how it should be.

Sorrow is mounting, the feeling of being **shattered.** Oppressive inner voices send me out into the desert. I don't know what's left to look for in this world. Total resignation. No sensation. No connectedness with my body. Scorn. The more I find myself, the more the night closes in around me.

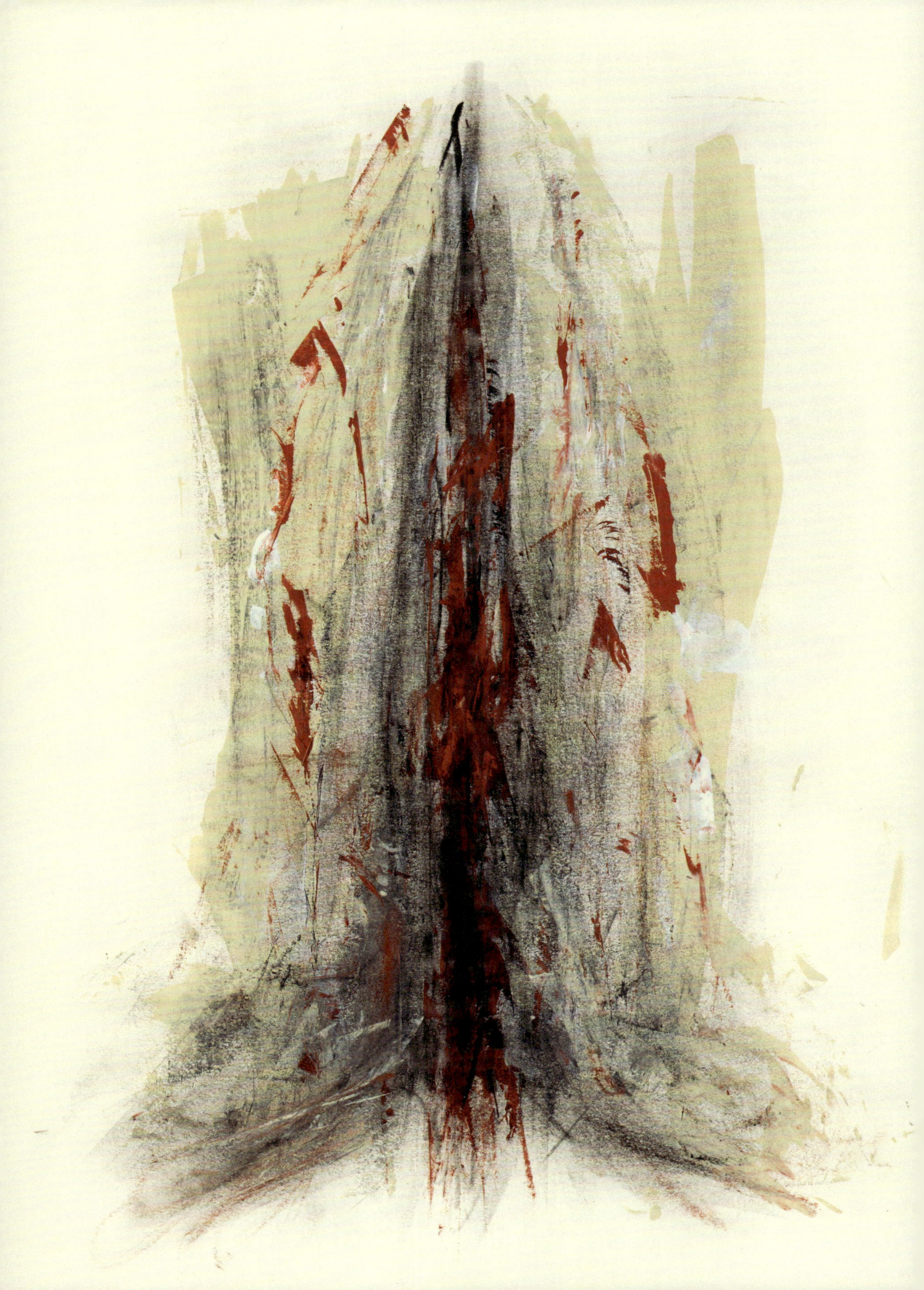

Forgiveness

Forgive oneself
and then
forgive others.

That's
the only way.

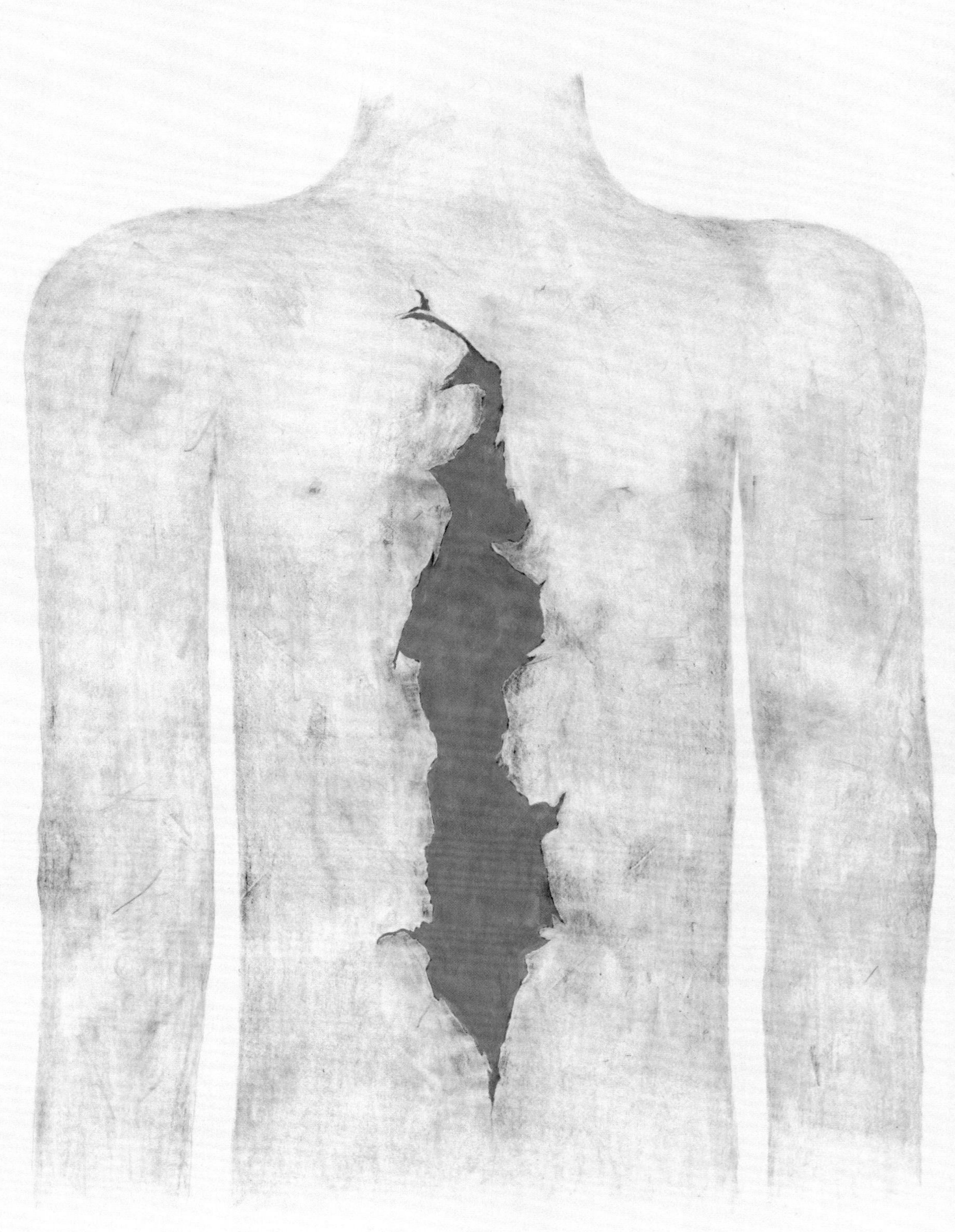

A gaping, bottomless abyss appears — and the question: Does anything make sense anymore? The inner void manifests itself outwardly. I lose my orientation. My steps grow smaller, I withdraw into the hidden, magical, fairytale realms of my childhood, a world which brings relief and a quiet, almost silent, sensual type of joy. I am sad because I don't feel needed.

I am lying in an entrance hall and am being abused. I rise out of my body, notice my heart, and see myself from above. Time and motion have stopped, there is only a frozen state of being. Silence. Alone again. The surroundings shift, I am being led. It is somber and an overwhelming stupor overcomes me. A red light burns on the floor. I see children, naked and seemingly lifeless, hanging vertically. Their bodies are attached, I feel their skin, their essence, their pain. Someone gives me a small, thin knife, like a dagger, leads me to one of them and, covering my hand on the handle, stabs the lower abdomen, between the legs. I am not present. I am not really there.

The room is full of angels. A picture depicts a child on an upside-down cross. It transforms itself into a butterfly. This butterfly is an angel.

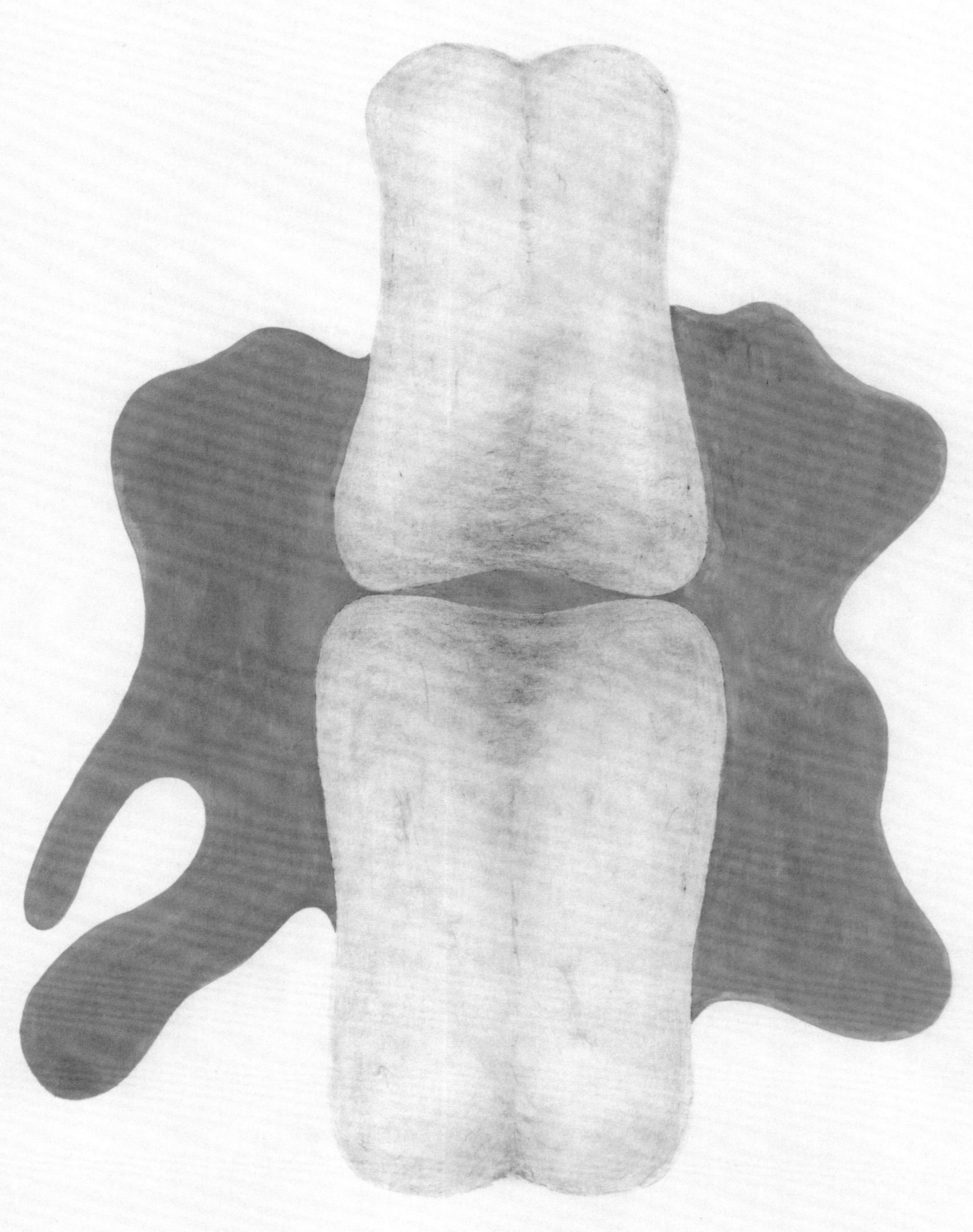

The streets are foreign to me. I move as if in empty space, am transported and delivered, taken by the hand by someone I don't know. Where I am being led, is to other places. It's another world.

The gate to a corridor opens. Men with animal heads on their shoulders ceremonially line up next to each other. A red light is burning in the dark. Children have to pass by the line of men. I am one of them.

My hands and feet are bound together, everything seems gray and black. Loneliness is a cold grip taking hold of me, a dirty sheet, a bottomless pit. I am being molested and exhale the air through my slightly opened mouth. My lips notice the flow of air. I invite butterflies to come and play.

A naked woman steps forward to participate in the rites of the group. I witness a forced act of consummation of a marriage. I must remain present, fulfil a role. Blood flows as a sacrifice takes place. A phrase from my dreams stays with me: "Women with a higher consciousness must subjugate themselves to this sacrament." Fear resides in me and breathes my breath. When will fear turn into love?

Hands attend to me, on me, inside me. Thick black cloth cascades nearby. I am wearing short pants that are too tight and must move "well." Orders are given. I have detached these memories from the pain they have caused.

The world around me is lively and inspiring. I turn towards the light, moving towards wholeness. My heart shows me the way. I have come to stay.

I can describe chambers and corridors of a building. In each room something different is happening. Inanimate figures covered in blankets lie on the floor and are taken away. There is a wooden cross and there are men wearing hoods, whispers and the screams of children. I am wearing a shirt, underneath I am naked. I squeeze the throat of a girl next to me. She is not moving; I have no other choice. In a separate compartment a dark pool of water is embedded in the ground. Large hands and metal racks press bodies down under the water's surface.

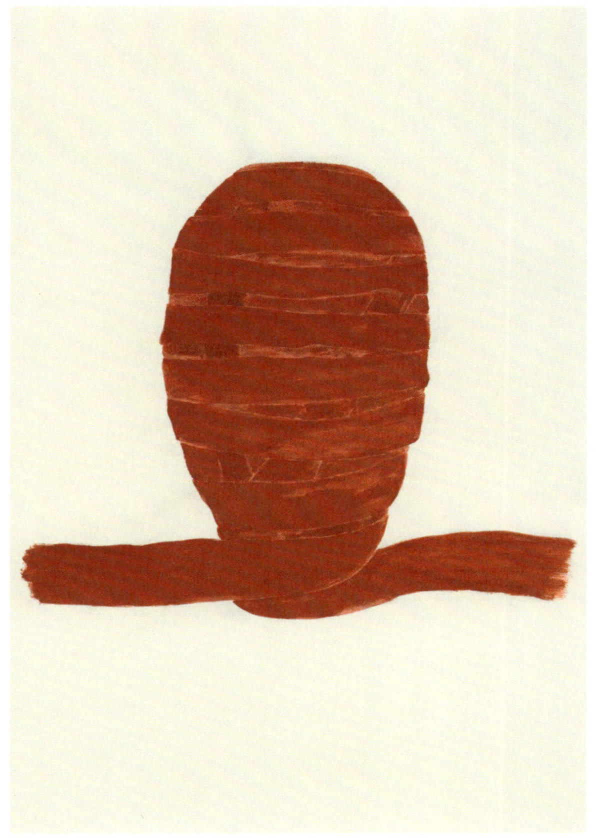

The tip of my nose touches the nose of another child, or maybe I am just dreaming this. So much silence.

My legs are trembling. A group of men are slaughtering three girls, and I must contribute to their suffering. A sketch shows me with the children. We are standing side by side without looking at each other. They are buried in the woods. I try to run away, am caught and punished. I can't breathe. I have angel wings and can view my human shell from above. I start to fly.

Because of my repeated attempts to escape, a world closes behind me. I often dream of freeing the other children and of burning everything down.

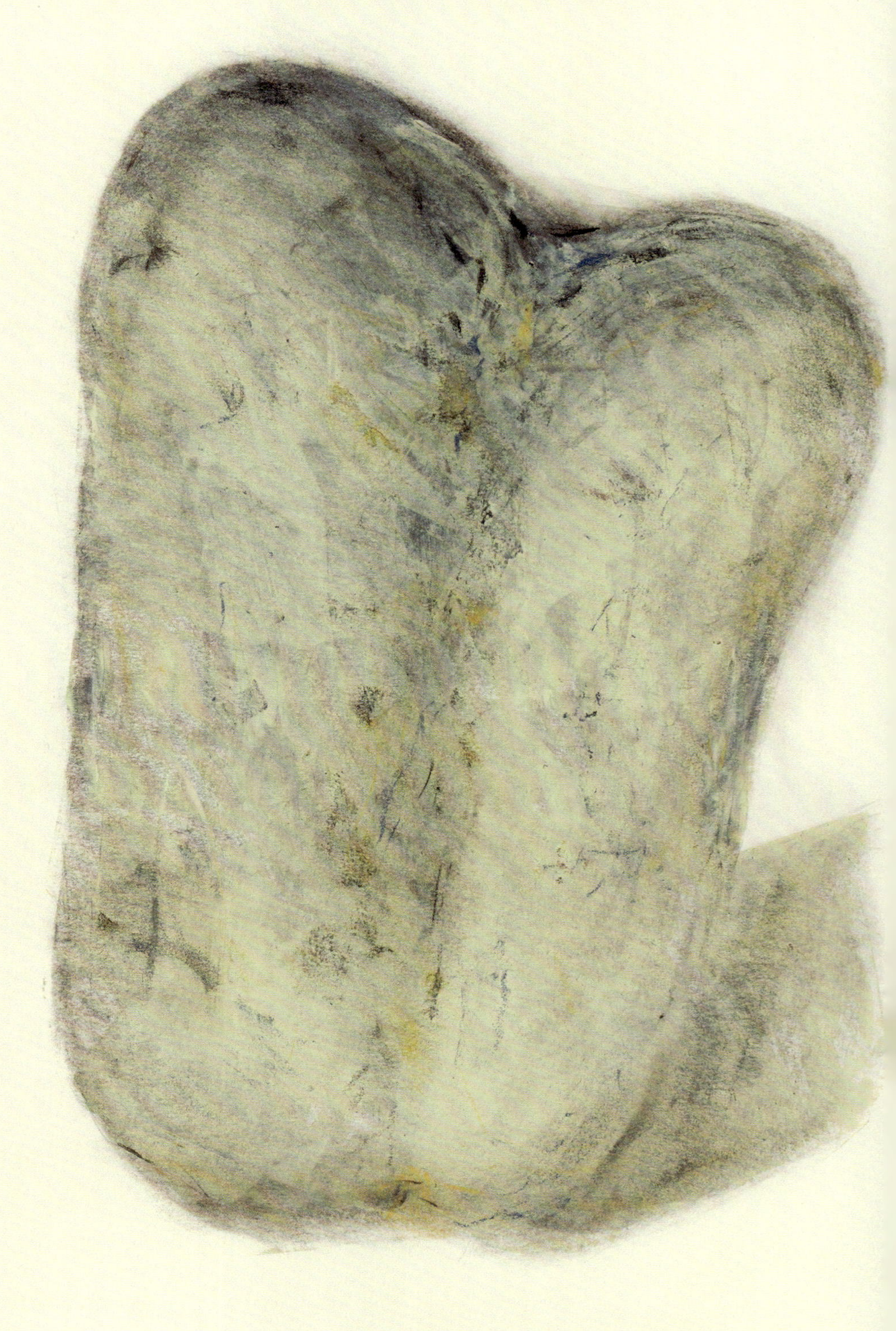

Every inner impulse is met with punishment. It is forbidden to show emotions. I would like to peel off my body like a glove and throw it out the window. Everything about me is bad and I have contributed to the torment of others.

I am held captive for satanic rituals. Judgment and humiliation follow me like shadows. Incomprehensible voices add to my isolation. This world is far removed from anything that can be seen as acceptable.

The blood of an infant flows towards a man in a black robe. I see a headless torso and numerous arms and other limbs lying side by side. Today I know that many children died and others were allowed to live, depending on their origins. I see the wounded, suffering, dying bodies but cannot absorb their agony. How I wish I could connect on a heart-level to give testimony about everything that happened. I would like to light candles and send paper ships with their names into the water.

I reveal myself exactly as I am and begin to heal in all colors and facets. Life opens up a radiant door for me. I walk through and stand in the light.

It's a new day
and I say to myself:
Nothing more can happen.
It's over.

To no longer breathe,
no longer feel… to block
all sensation means
to survive. And yet, to
not breathe is an inner
death, a withdrawal
from life, from aliveness
and light.

Encounters, touch,
being seen by
other people — how
frightening! The idea
of a happy life terrifies
me. I am accustomed
to limitations and
resignation… To make
an effort, neverthe-
less?… This feels like
jumping off a bridge
and somehow trusting
that a safety cord
will gently break my
fall. To trust in life,
is that possible?

I want to experience
and to be amazed.
How curious I am about
life. How curious!
I am here in this world
and I am whole.

So few kind words
apply to my existence.
The only thing I desire
is to rest. I feel half
dead, there is no escape.
This is all too much
for me. I punch myself;
my body is deaf and
dumb. I throw more
and more punches; with
each blow, I distance
myself even more from
this existence. The
demon has won; it is
tearing me to pieces.
Maybe that's how it
should be.

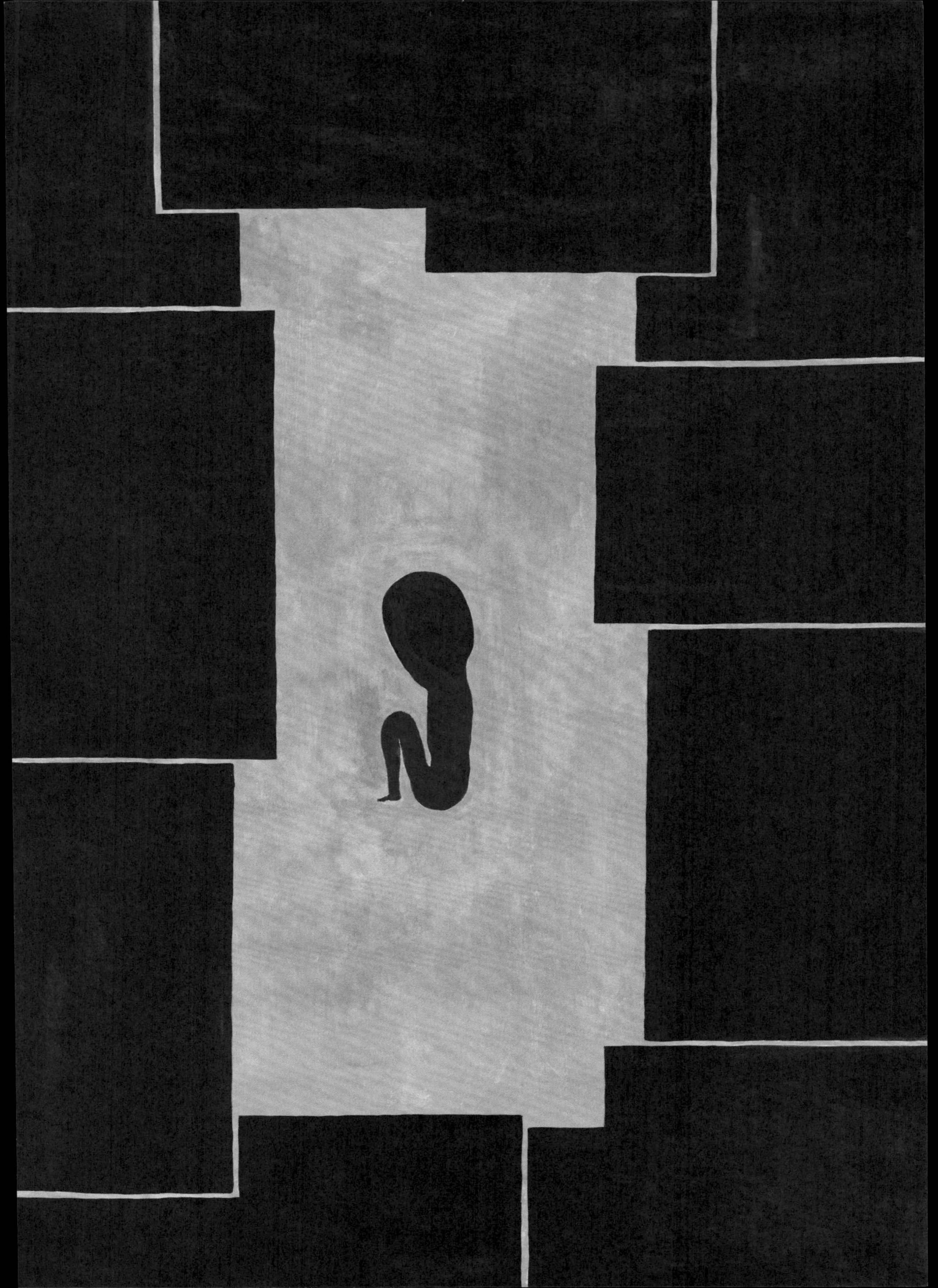

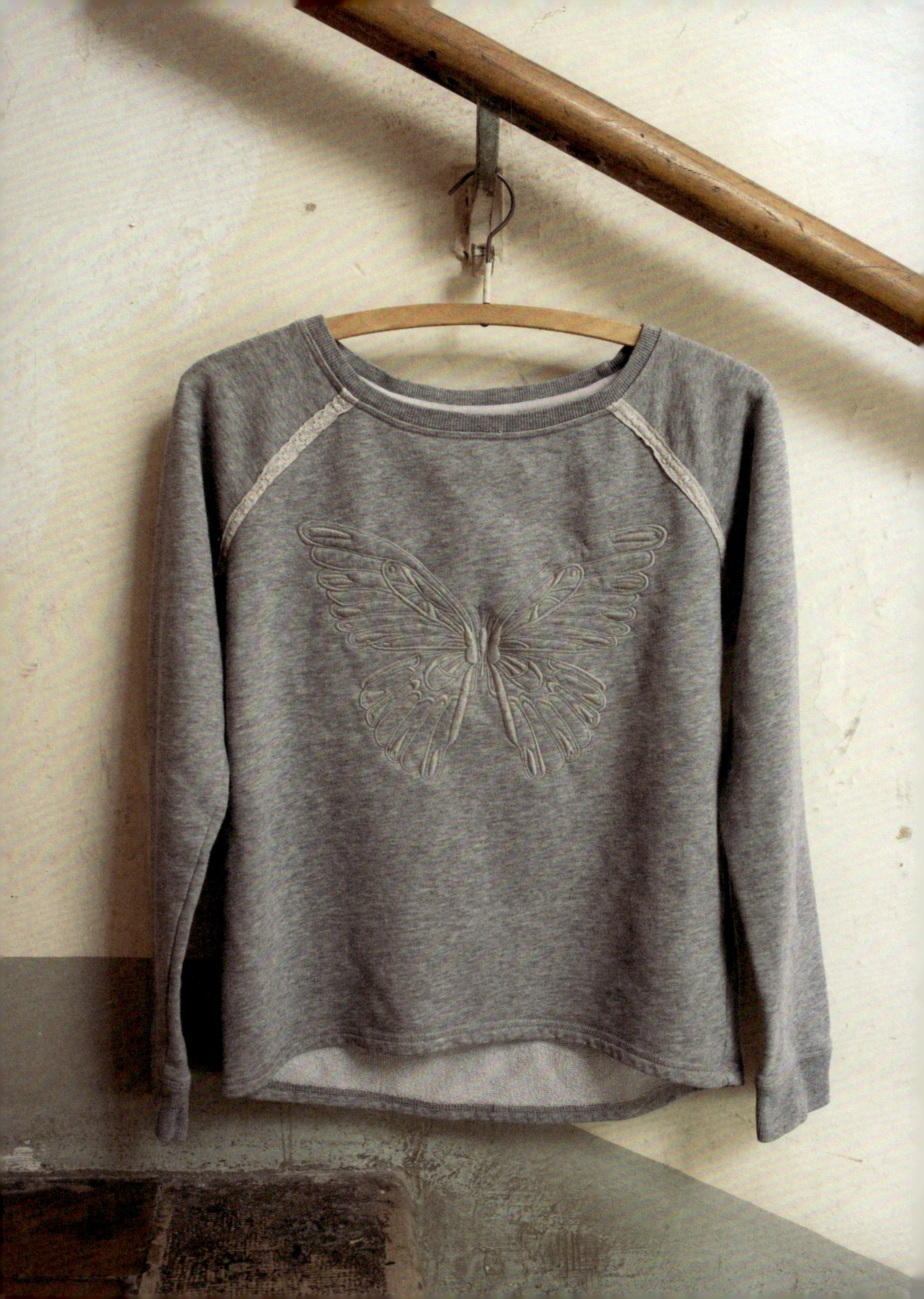

Isolation is the worst. I go home and no one cares. When I see couples who have a deep connection, it feels like the world spit me out.

Yesterday, I noticed a butterfly on a child's sweater. The wings that were stitched onto gray cloth were pleasant to touch. They had a vibrant presence as if, through synchronicity, they were an expression of the experiences of the heart.

I hear a voice like an echo that says: "Who do you think you are? Do you really think you are all that special? What are you trying to prove with all these tall tales? Nobody believes you anyway. You had the best childhood!"

I am invited to a clothes swap and appear in other clothing. This reminds me of what happened some time before, and of the girls' dress that I didn't want to wear but was forced to. An inner image shows a fabric that is placed over me but underneath I am naked. I see the color red, a dress with open slits, like a big net that reveals more than it conceals. I feel nauseous, struggle for air. There are people, mostly men, around me. I want to hide from sight somewhere on the side but remain in the center.

My mother kicks my head, with outstretched arms, over and over. I cringe, try to protect myself. Were there ever any good moments?

When was I ever really happy? I don't know… I don't have any such memories. There were no festivities, no time was spent with joyful people. I played by myself. I remember that my behavior at school attracted negative attention. If children are sexually violated, when and how does it begin? My strongest memory from my primary school days is of having oral sex with a classmate. Was I sold to have sex with men? Was I caught up in ritual pedophile worlds?

A child is being strangled, fights back, and tries to protect itself. After the strangling comes the stabbing, then the slashes. Blood flows. The children bleed out as they hang there, one body next to another. I can't bear seeing this image that is stuck in my mind, I can't stand it anymore.

The fabric of the dress is bright red, damp, clingy. I see myself in this state, petrified, aware of people on top of me and behind me. The dress is open from below and so am I.

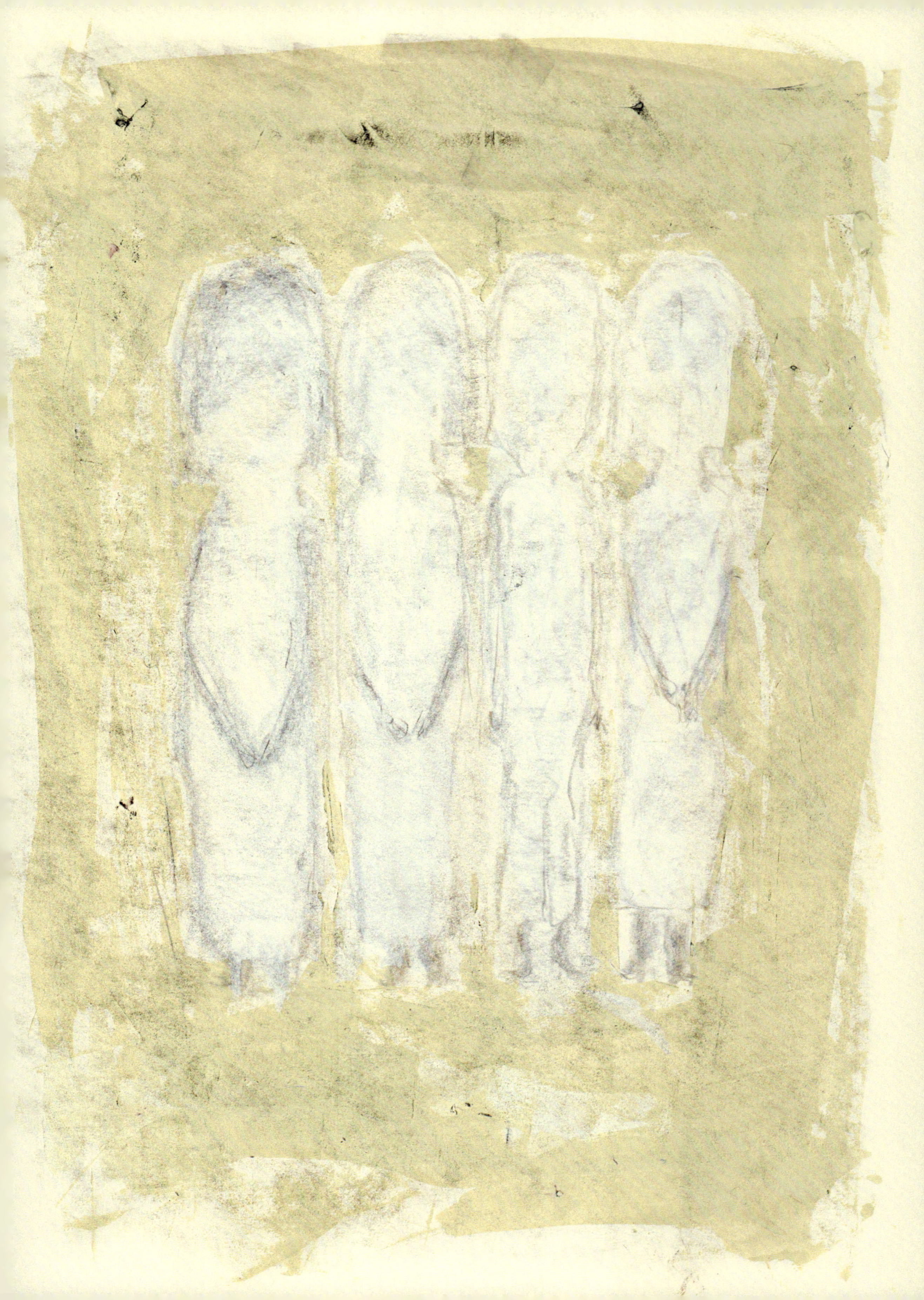

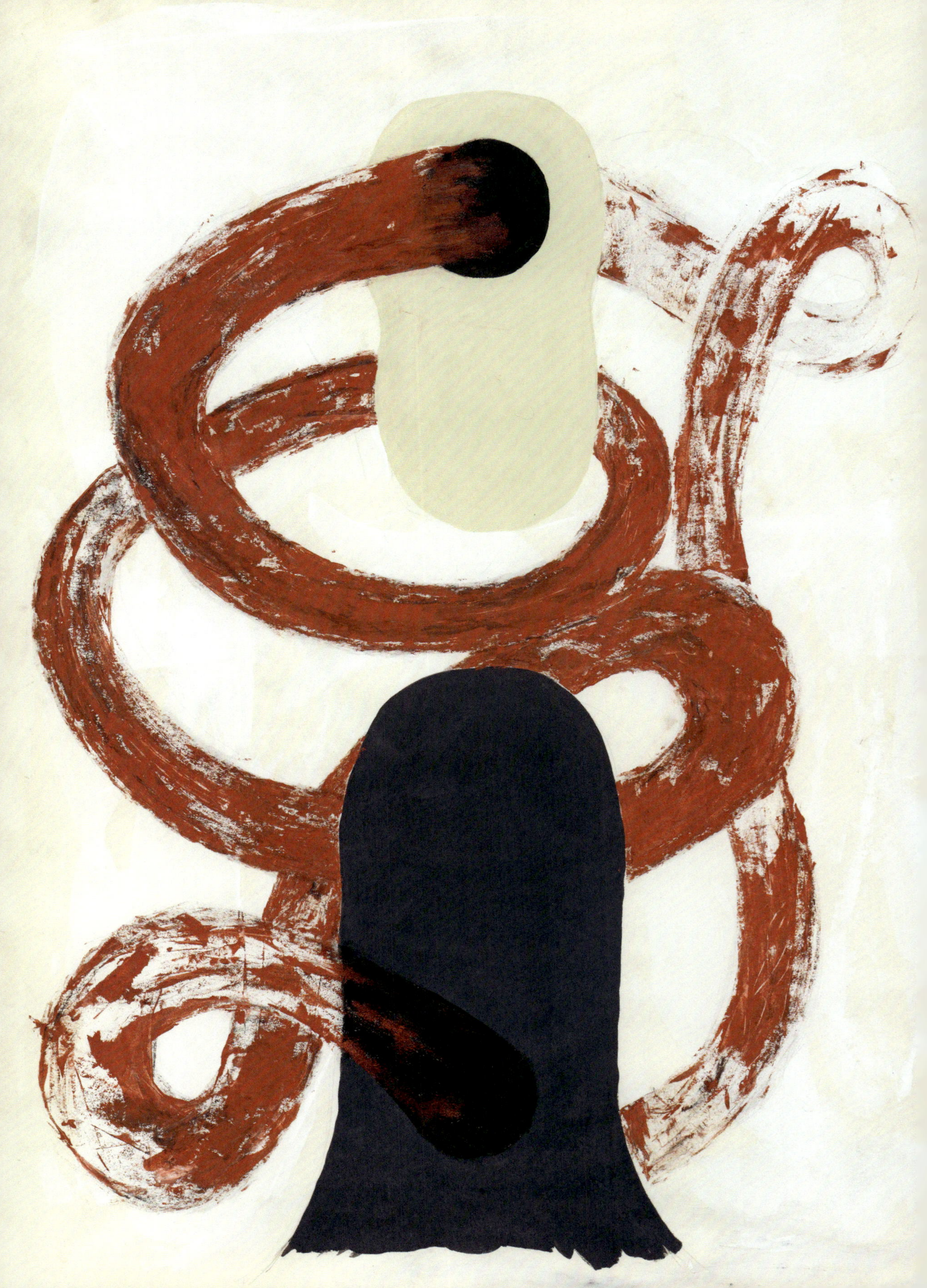

**A hunt is taking place
in an open field with trees.**

I am with other children.
The sun sets and we are told to run,
are caught and beaten.
I can hardly run, am afraid,
and feel how my arms
are being tied behind my back.

My head is pushed
into something warm, something soft,
it's hard for me to breathe.
I hide under a blanket,
close my eyes.

My inner child takes me by the hand,
leads me down corridors.
I begin to realize
that I know some of those children.

My eyes are directed towards the ground
in the hope that I will not be noticed,
that I will not be seen.

We undress,
receive something to drink,
put on other clothes,
and are sexually assaulted.

Where was my father?

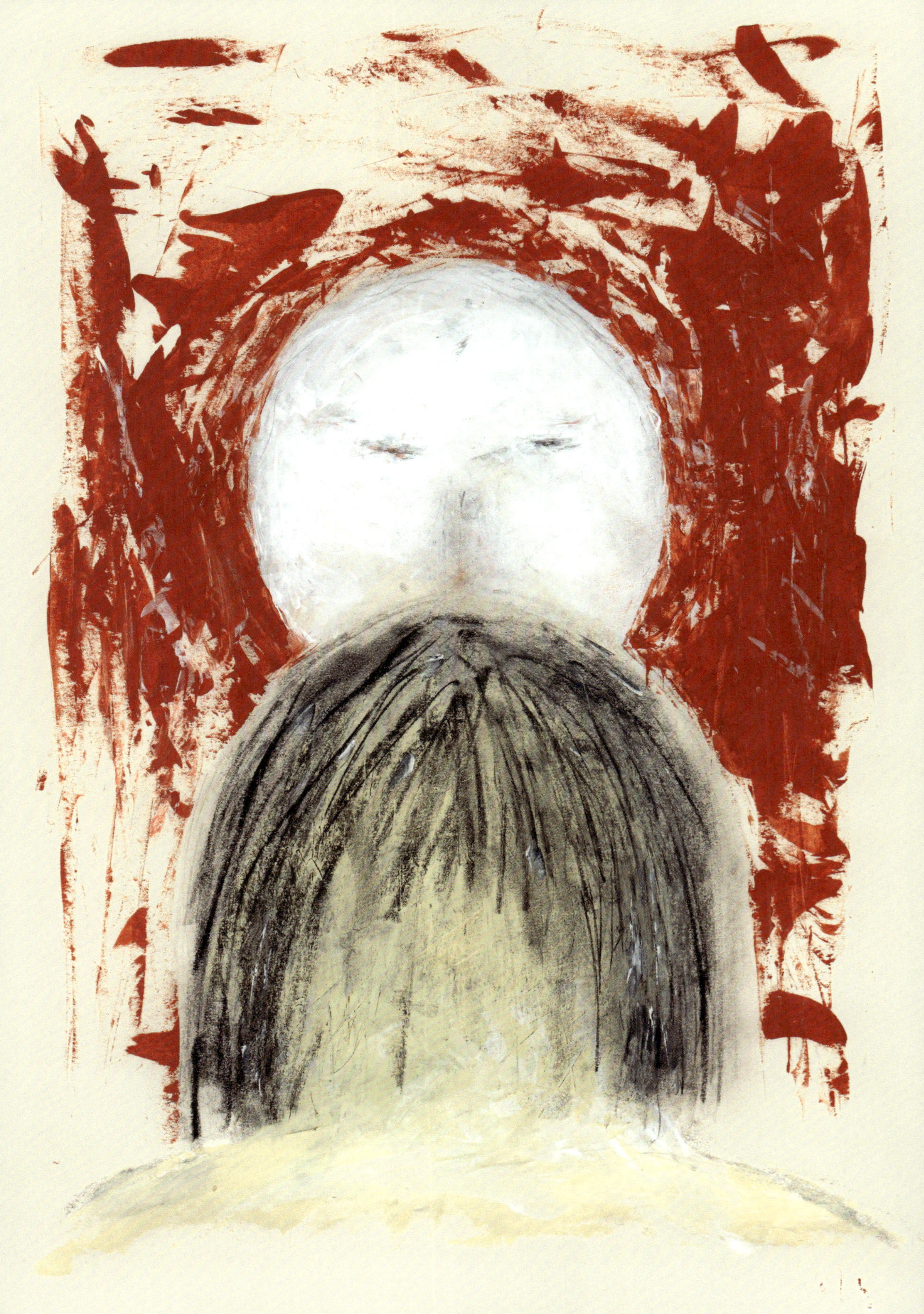

Once again the memory of a children's home comes to mind, an old house with dim walls, on a hill of the city. Years later, a commission was formed to shed light on the horrors that were suffered there. Mounted pictures lurk motionless in the night. That's how deeply these events remain buried.

My hips are tightly grasped. The stomach of a child is sliced open as part of a ritual. I become aware of intestines, blood, the child's genitals are also mutilated. Everything is red; an emptied-out, disfigured being is lying so close to me. Then the throat is slit and I see how the shoulders and head sink in a sea of dark liquid.

My feet are trembling upwards, into the center of my heart, into my dreams.

I learn to cope with being alone. Why does my past keep coming back to show its dark face? Is there something I'm supposed to say? There was a small number of men who I call high priests. Girls were sacrificed, their hearts cut out. The bodies that were buried had no core anymore. I did not want to be separated from these children; I would have wanted to stay with them.

As a boy, deprived of safe and protective relationships, I obeyed orders. I agreed to go along with everything as long as it allowed me to cling onto a tiny bit of life. I don't know exactly what that was. That tiny bit was chiseled away more and more until there was nothing left. I fell apart, maybe when I was four years old. I told myself that I am not that child.

I left myself behind in order to stay alive. I left myself behind. There was no other choice.

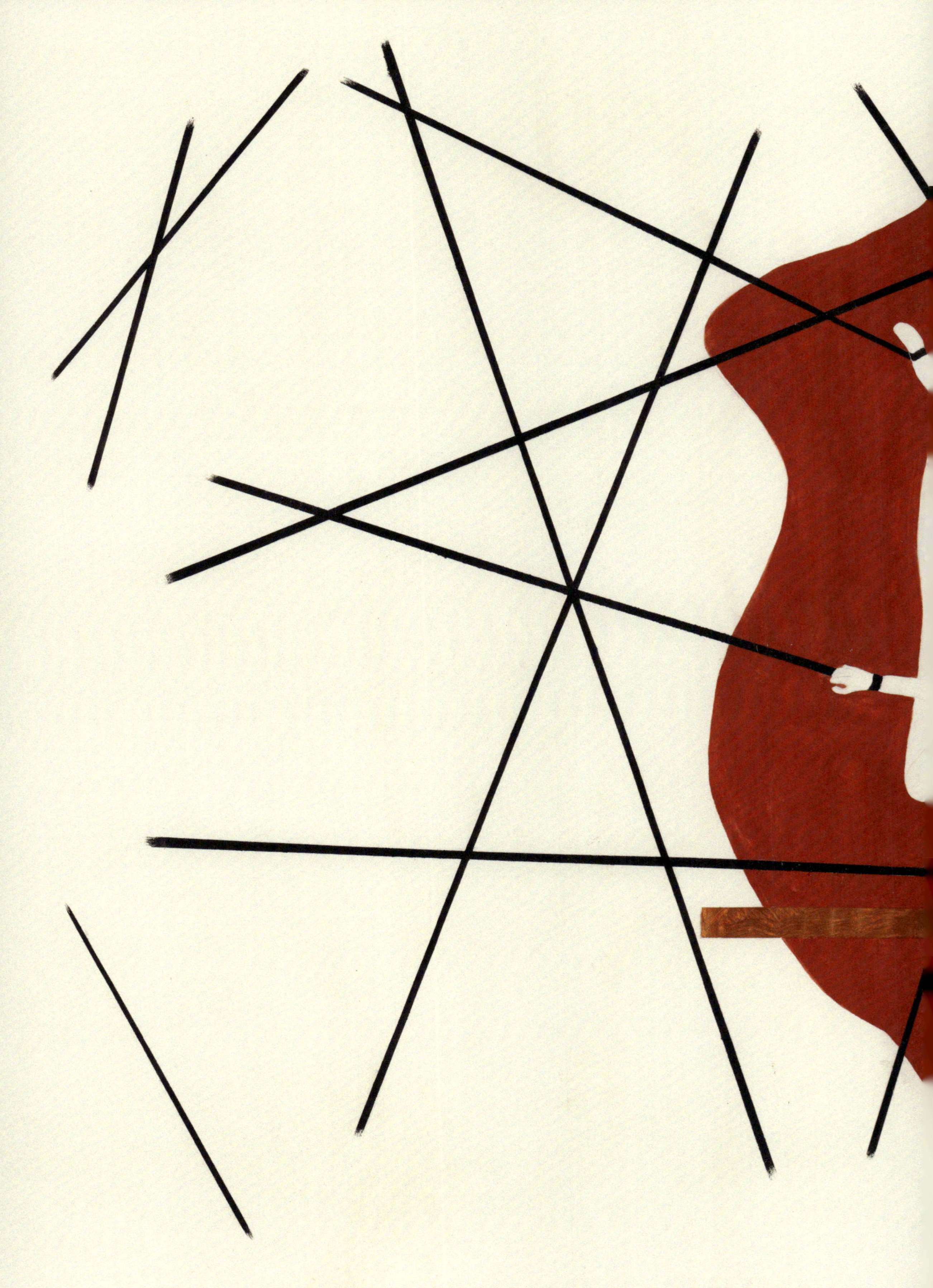

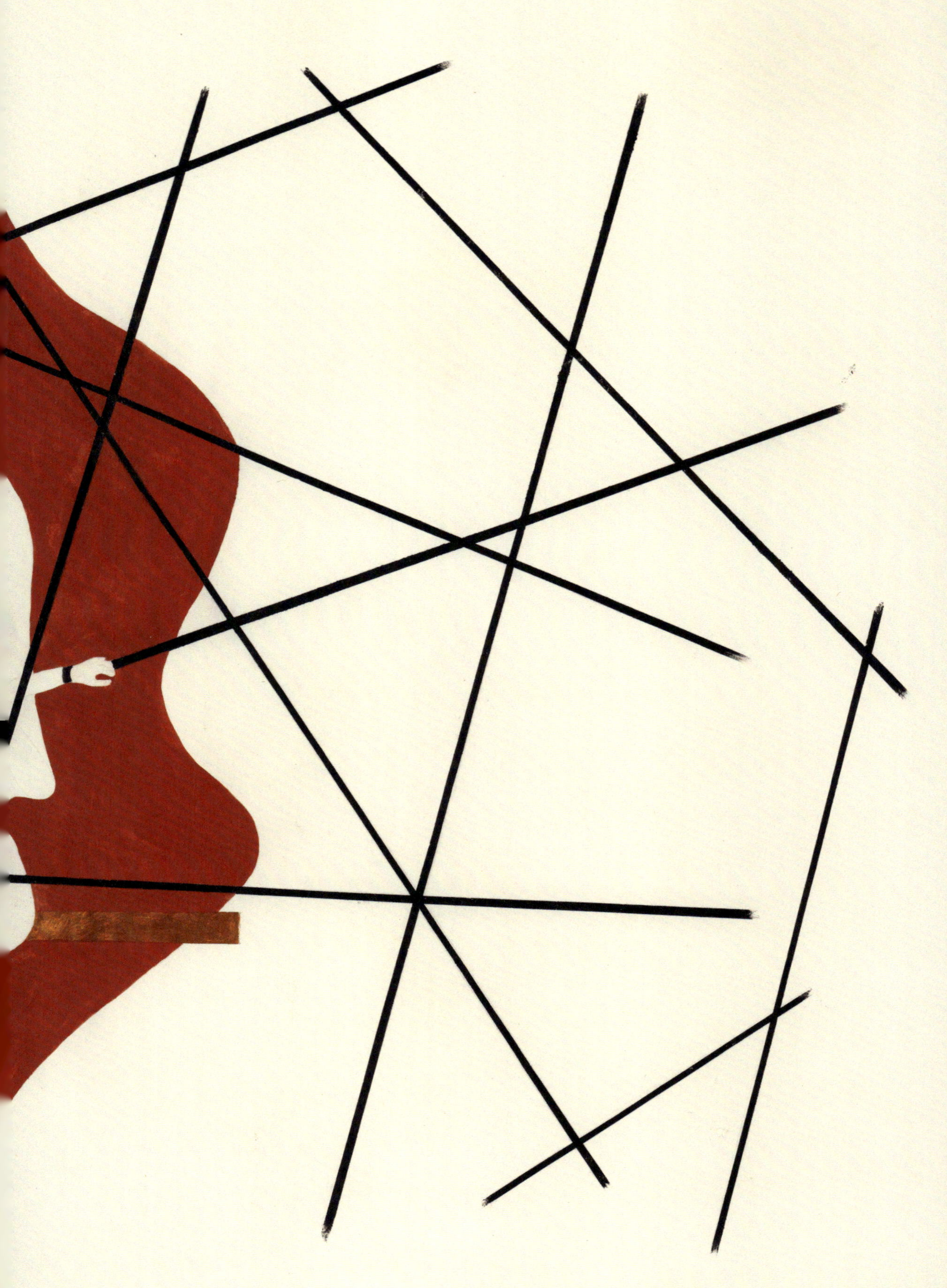

The body divides itself
into several segments.
Some permit entry,
others fade into the
distance. I bring
with me a quiet and
forlorn companion.

It all begins with me.
I appear in a woodland
clearing as a brightly
shining statue, standing
erect in the middle
of secluded woods.
I visualize a sea of colors
bringing light into the
darkness. My separate
parts approach me, each
with its own wounds.
They gather around me,
clamoring to enter
my world.

Am I still seeking
a place of refuge?
Have I stopped closing
doors, hoping that
they might reveal
a home or safe haven
behind them?

How do I handle my
yearning for a different
world?

I am that small child
who is determined
to break away courageously
from the dominion of power,
coercion, and the abuse
of body and spirit.
I am freeing myself from all limitations
and from the ties that bind me.

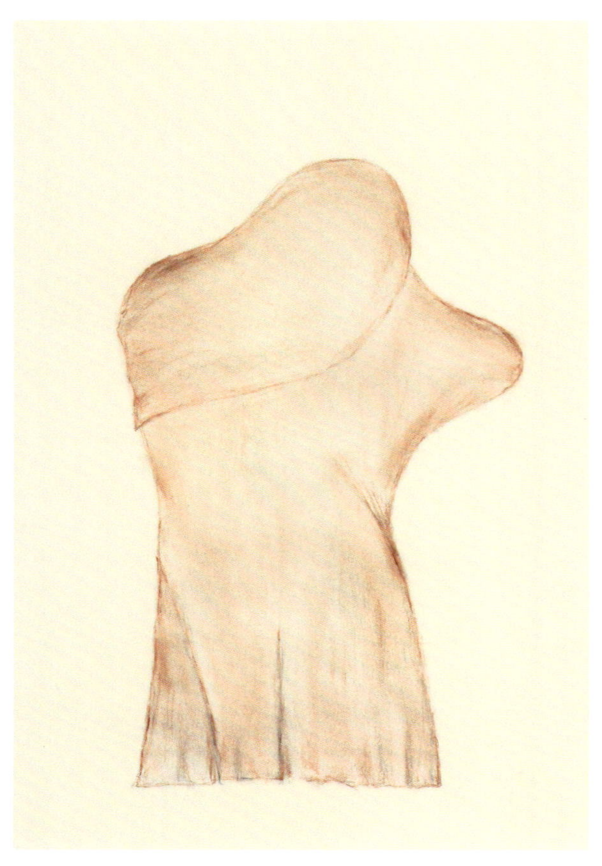
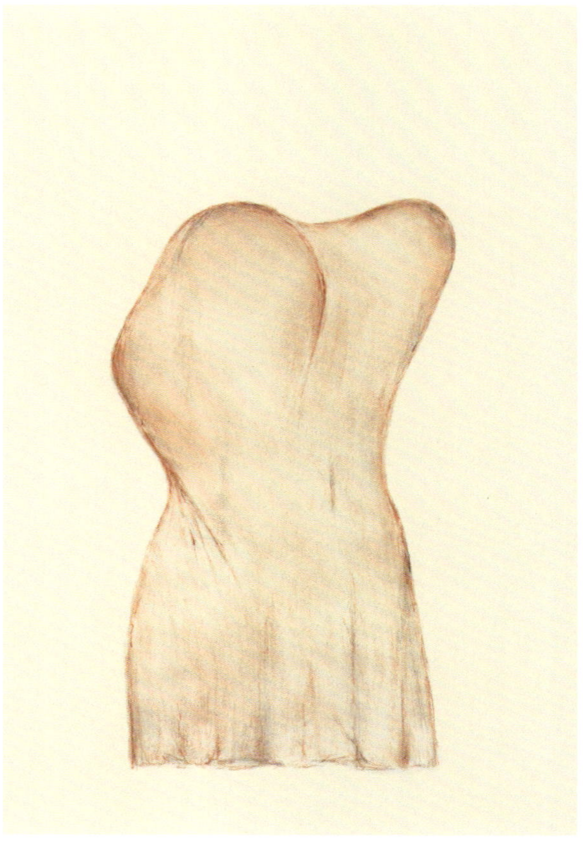

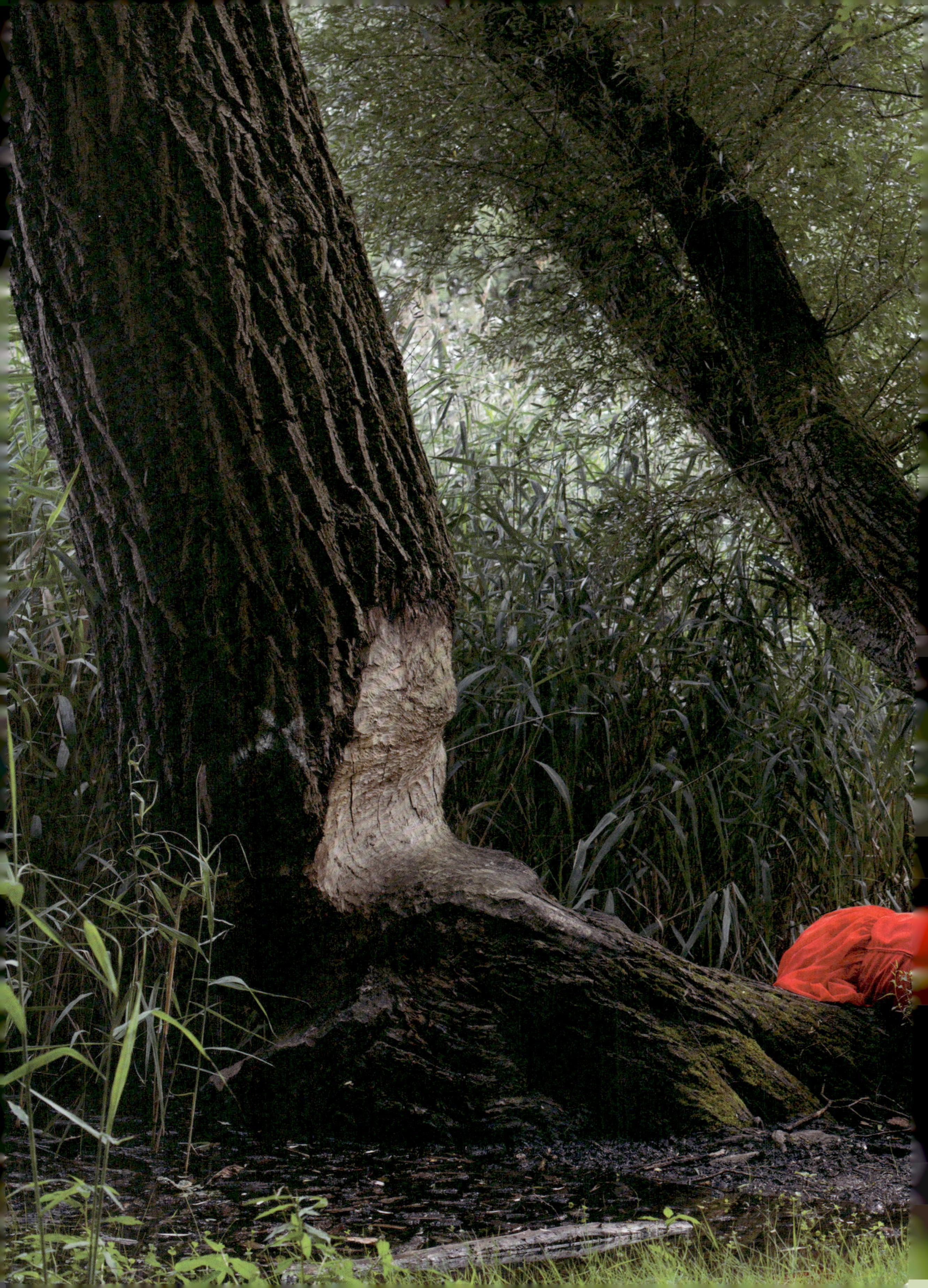

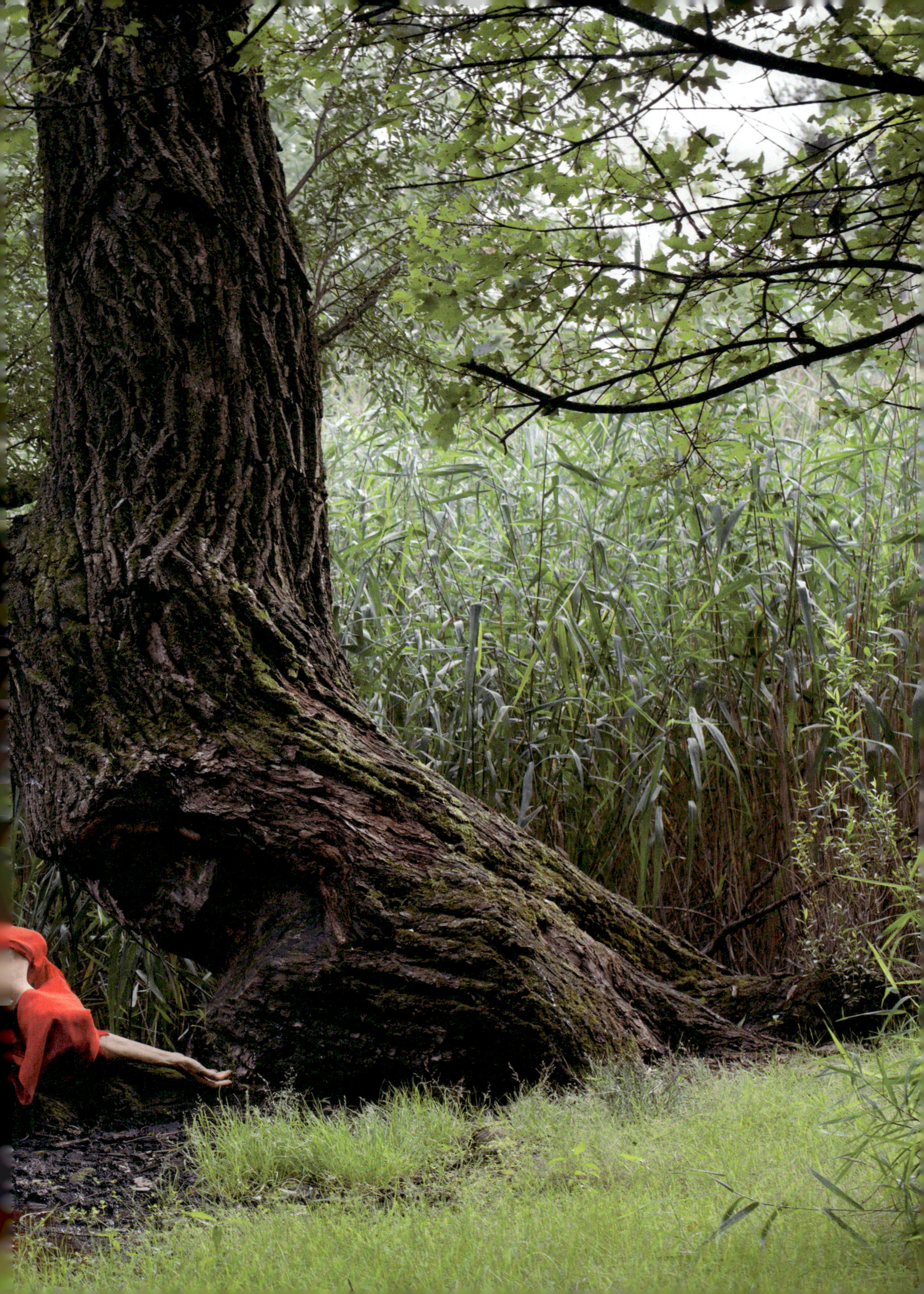

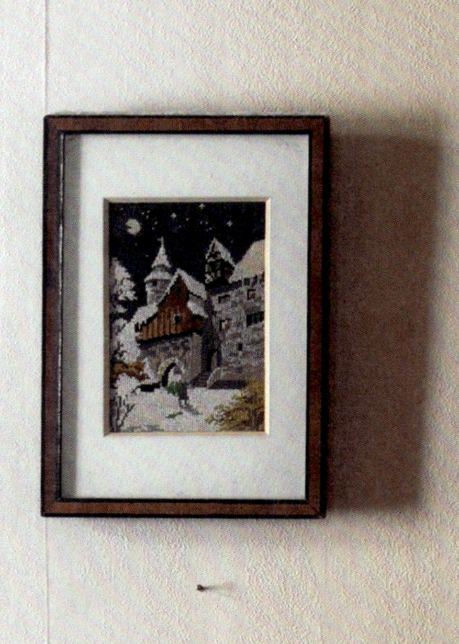

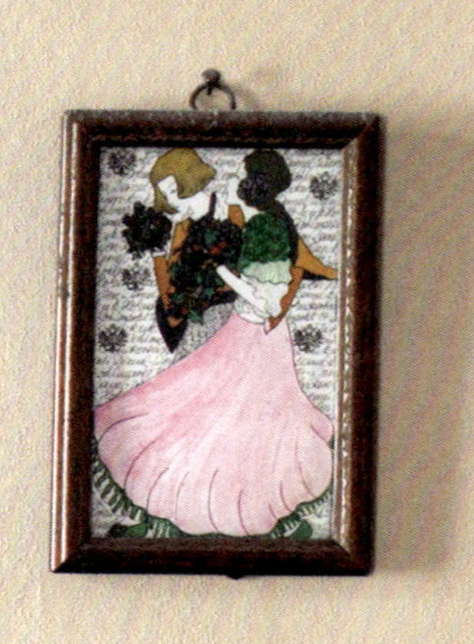

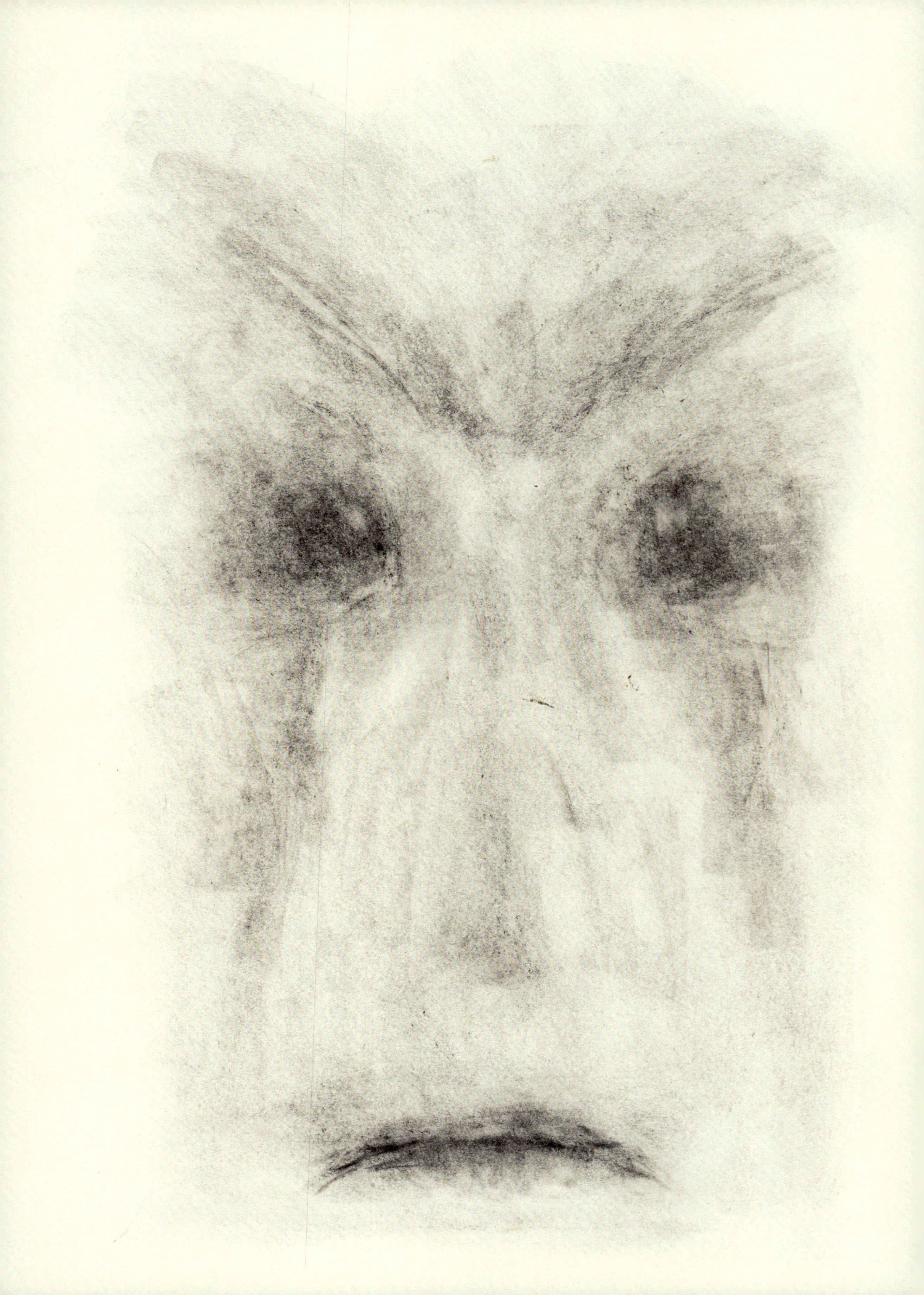

Rituals are held.

I see cloaked figures
and a person with a mask.
I must render service,
participate in decisions.
I am raped,
held tight and beaten,
coerced into killing.

I have to
pierce with a dagger,
drawing blood.
I see a toddler
pinned down on a table,
screaming.

I stand next to the men
and must watch.
Then all is silent.

I believe
that I was often present
on such occasions.

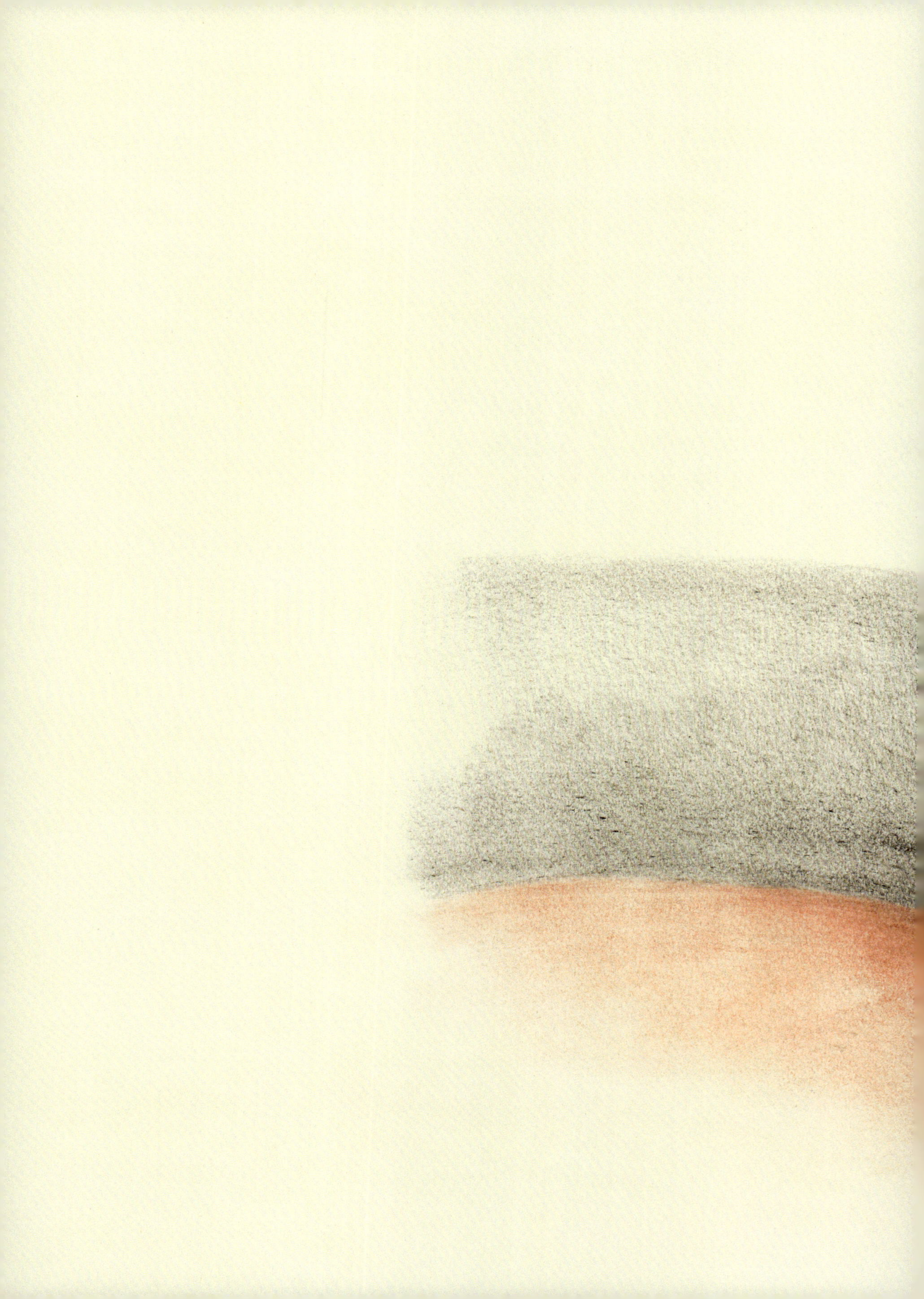

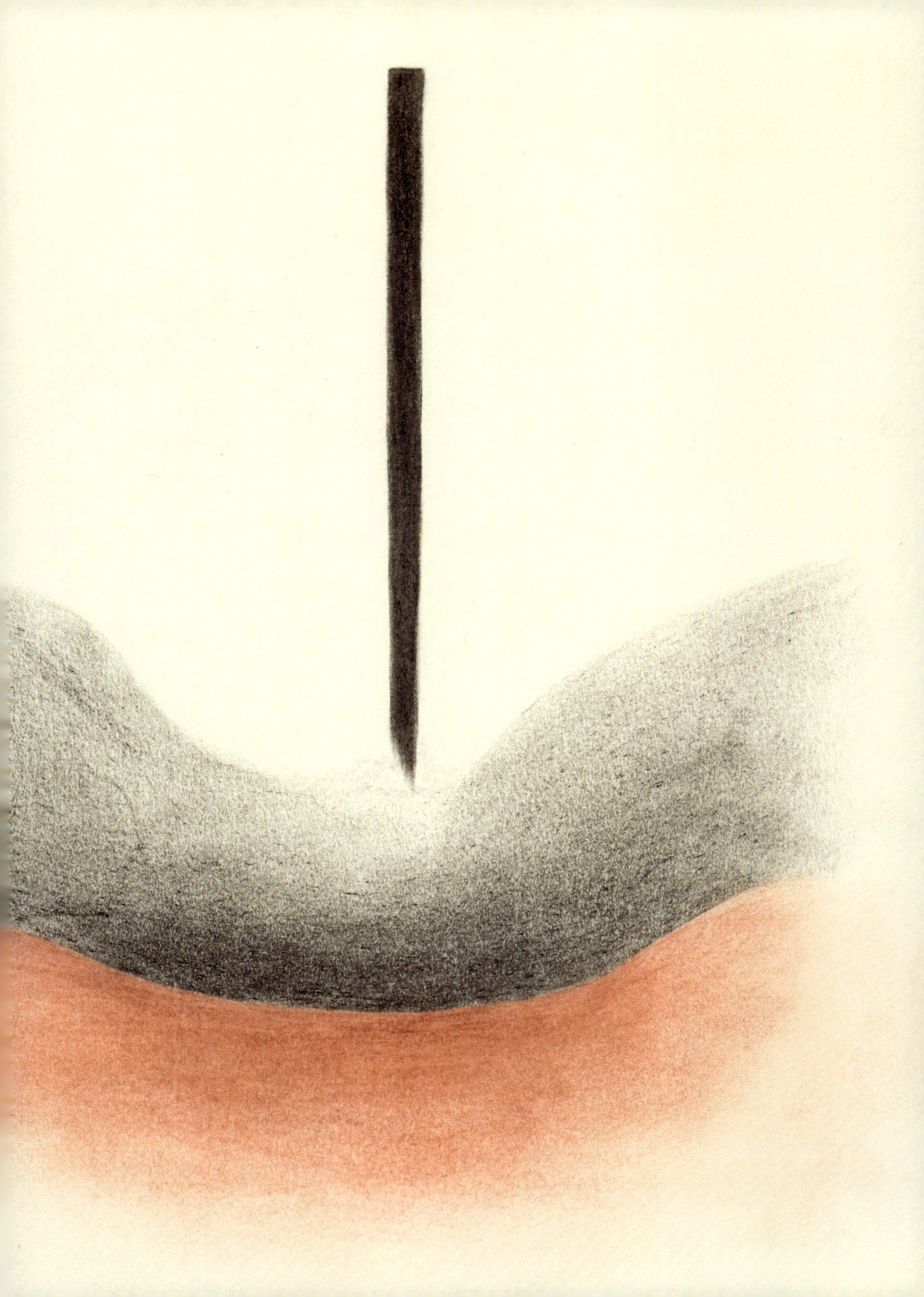

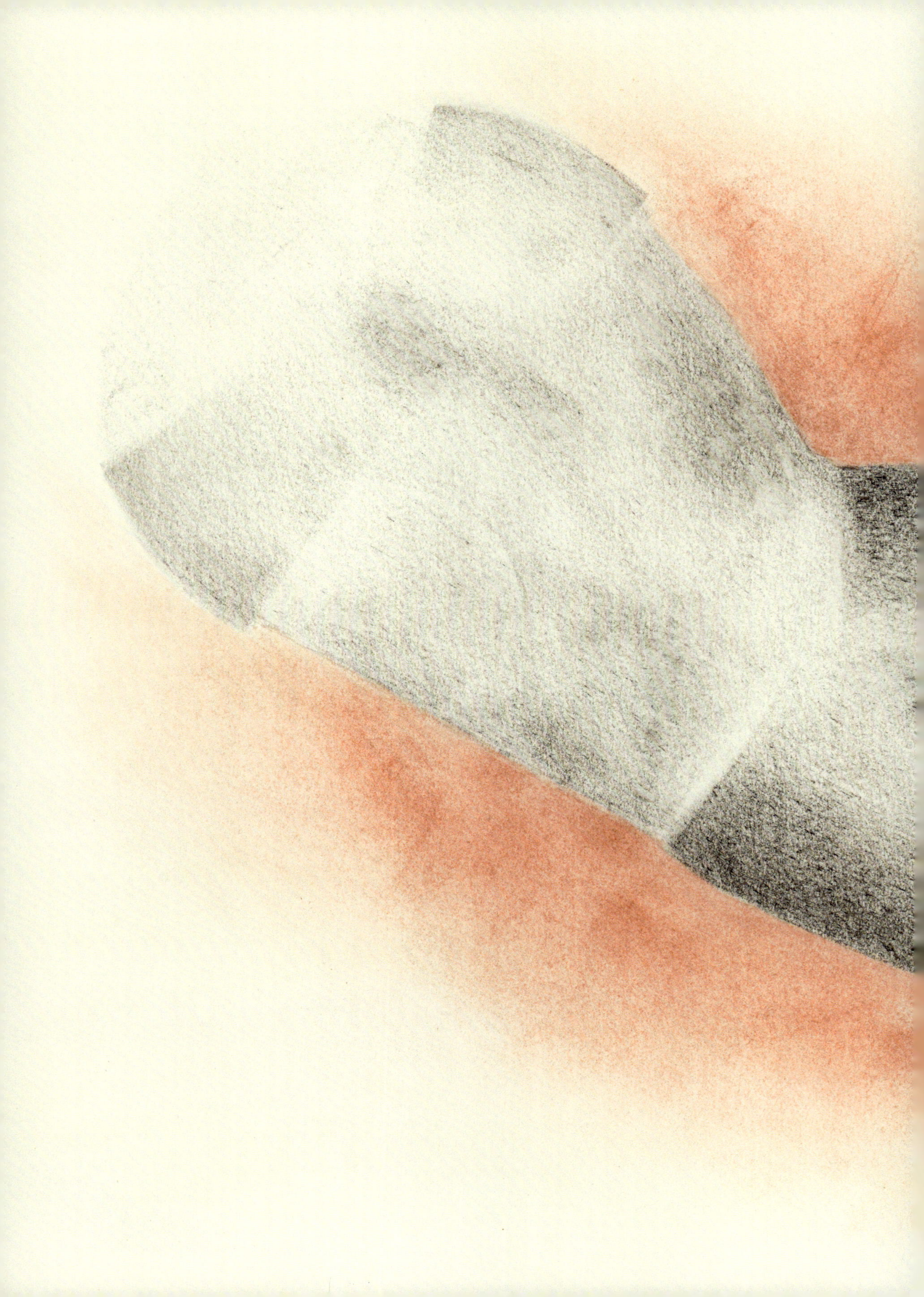

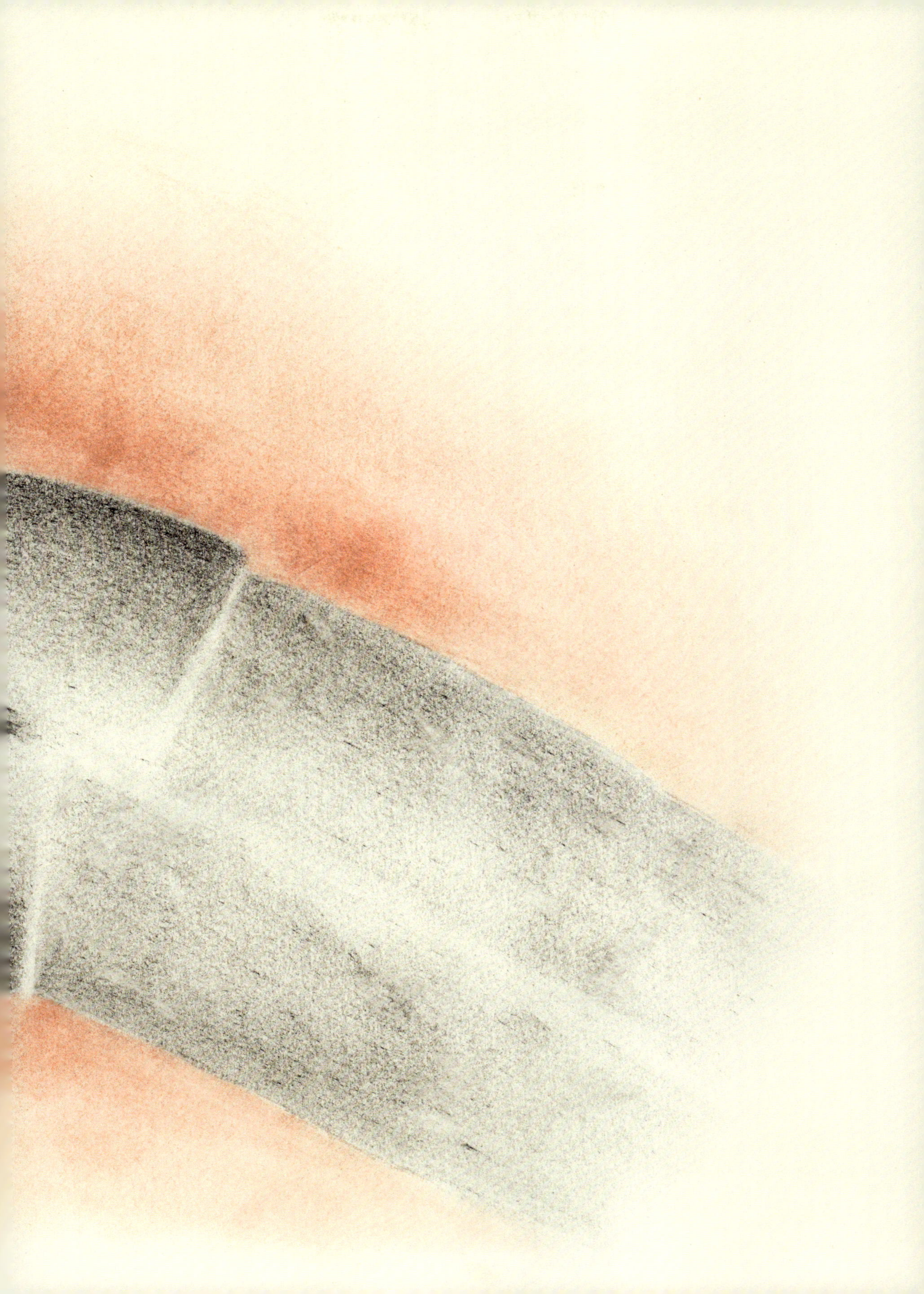

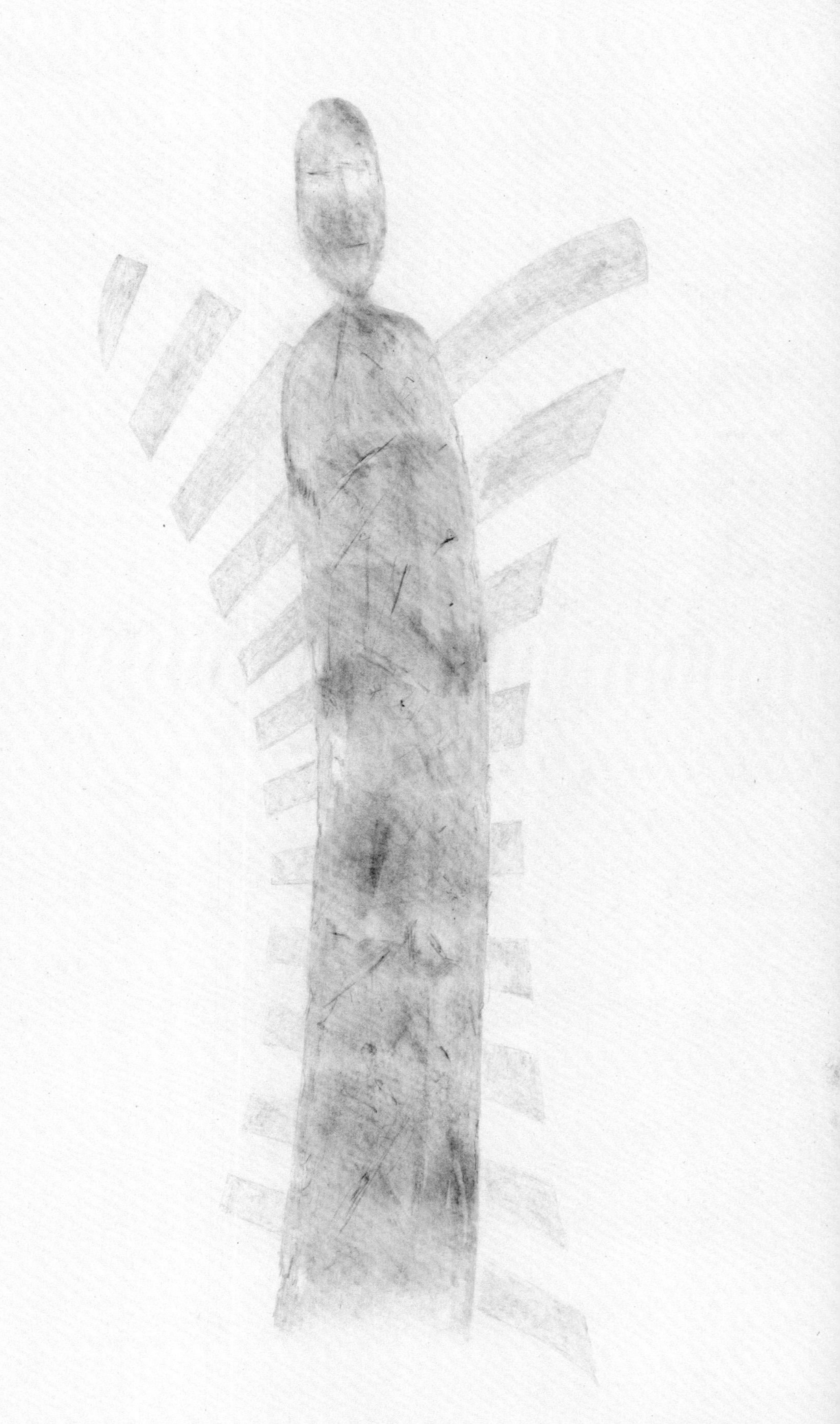

I am light.

I have experienced **all of this and much more.** I am not running away anymore from my past, as shadowy as it may be. I am growing back together into a person with a history and a soul. I choose to accept my life with love.

The self-infliction of injuries increases in brutality the deeper I go in this process. I see myself as mutilated, tied to a tree, isolated. In view of these images, I forfeit any right to my own existence.

Guardian spirits and friends support me unharmed into a life of freedom. Everything is already there. Old paradigms begin to lose their power as I work daily on visualizing a life filled with light.

To my inner child: You are beautiful inside and out. You are authentic and you are not to blame for your childhood experiences. You are full of light and light is your element. You no longer need to make yourself small and to hide in darkness. You can give that up forever. Retreating from life once served its purpose but now life is ready to receive you with open arms and to show you how beautiful you are. You may now let yourself be open.

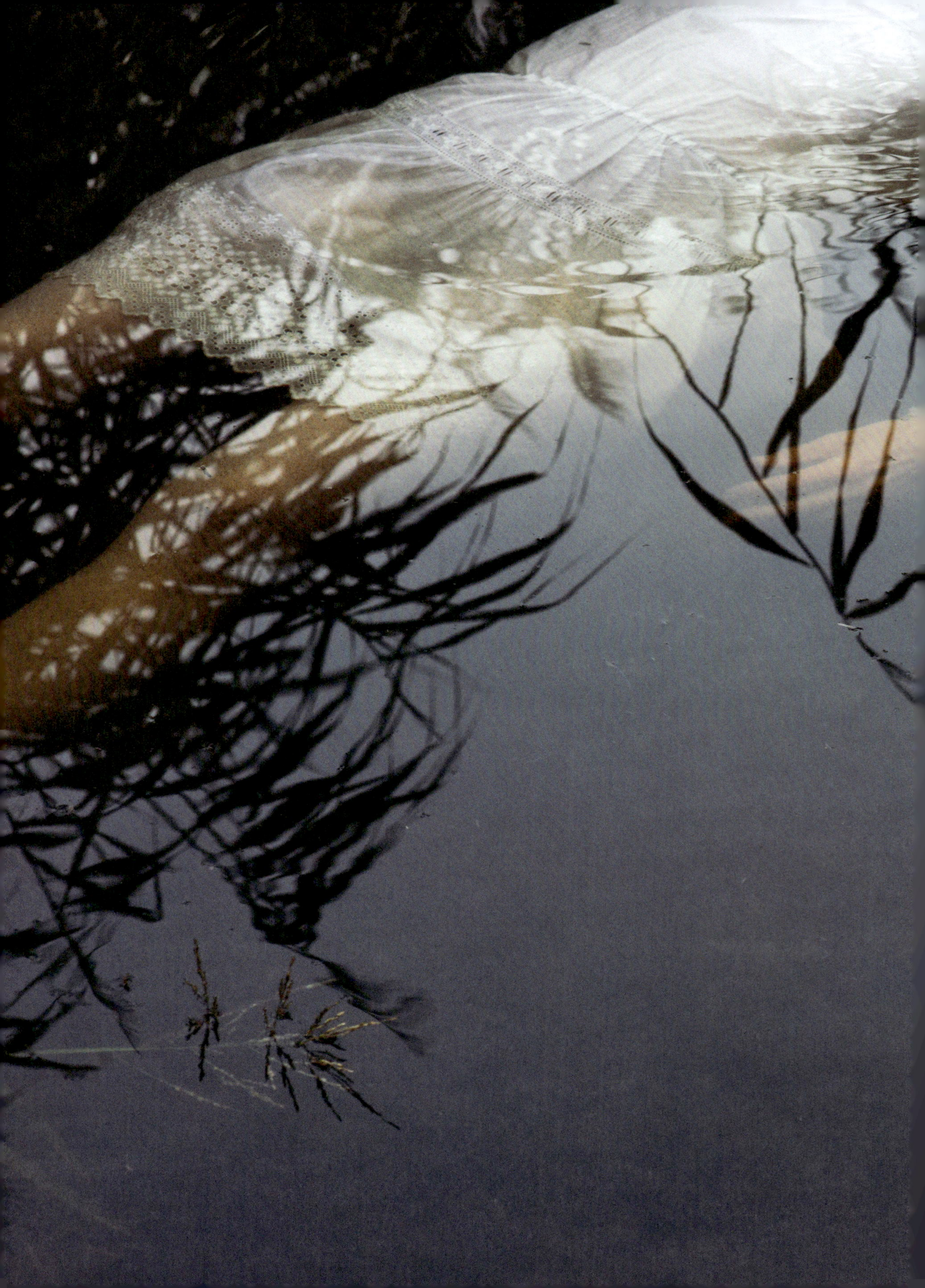

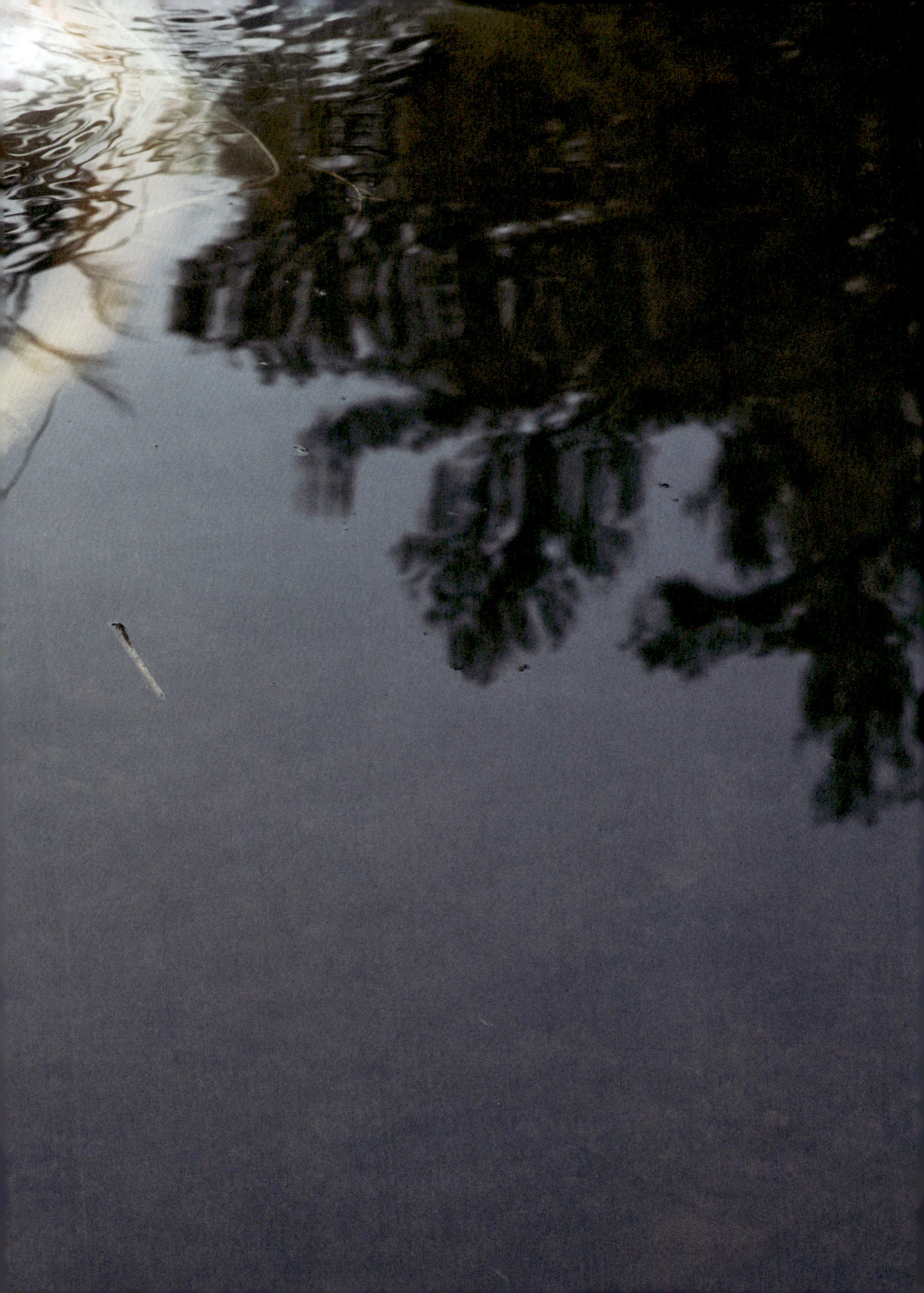

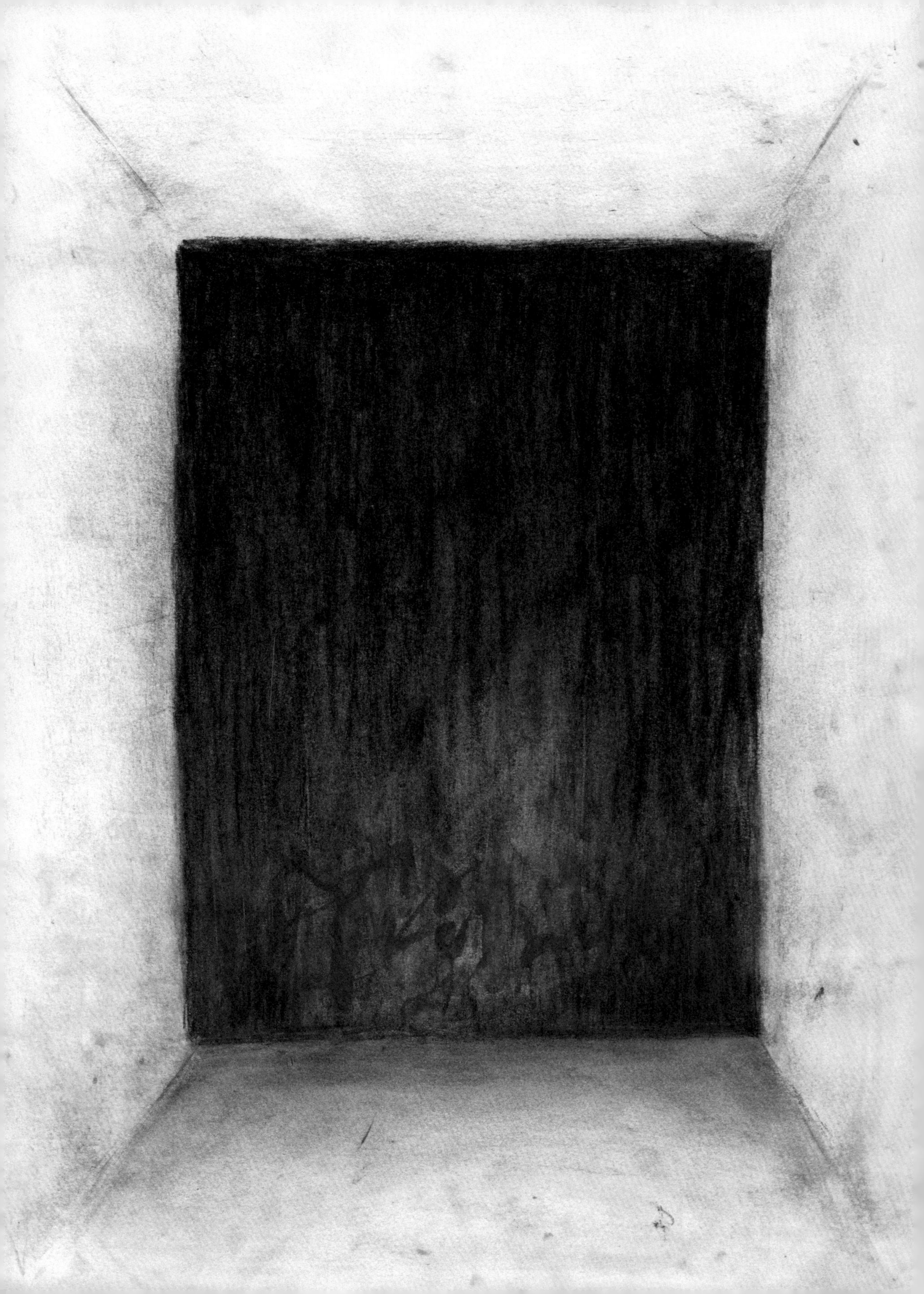

I see myself in a vehicle

heading for the countryside,
to the family of a schoolmate,
a plain house on the edge of the woods.
I wait in a room,
hear voices in the kitchen.

On the way into the cellar,
someone pulls down my pants.
Hands grab my lower body,
my upper body strikes the wall.

I am the victim
of a painful assault
with no way
to defend myself.

Somebody has "delivered me"
and has been paid for this.

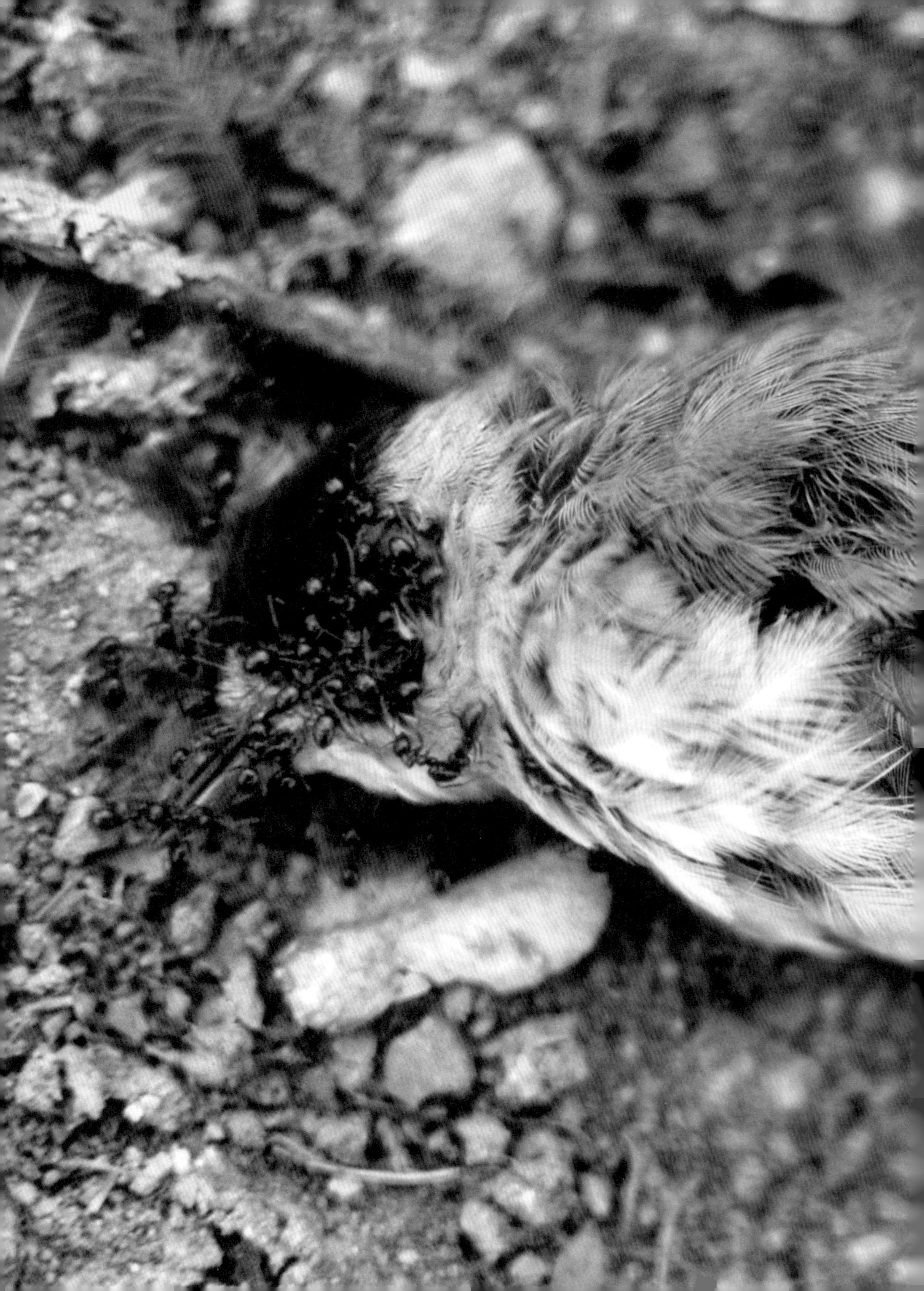

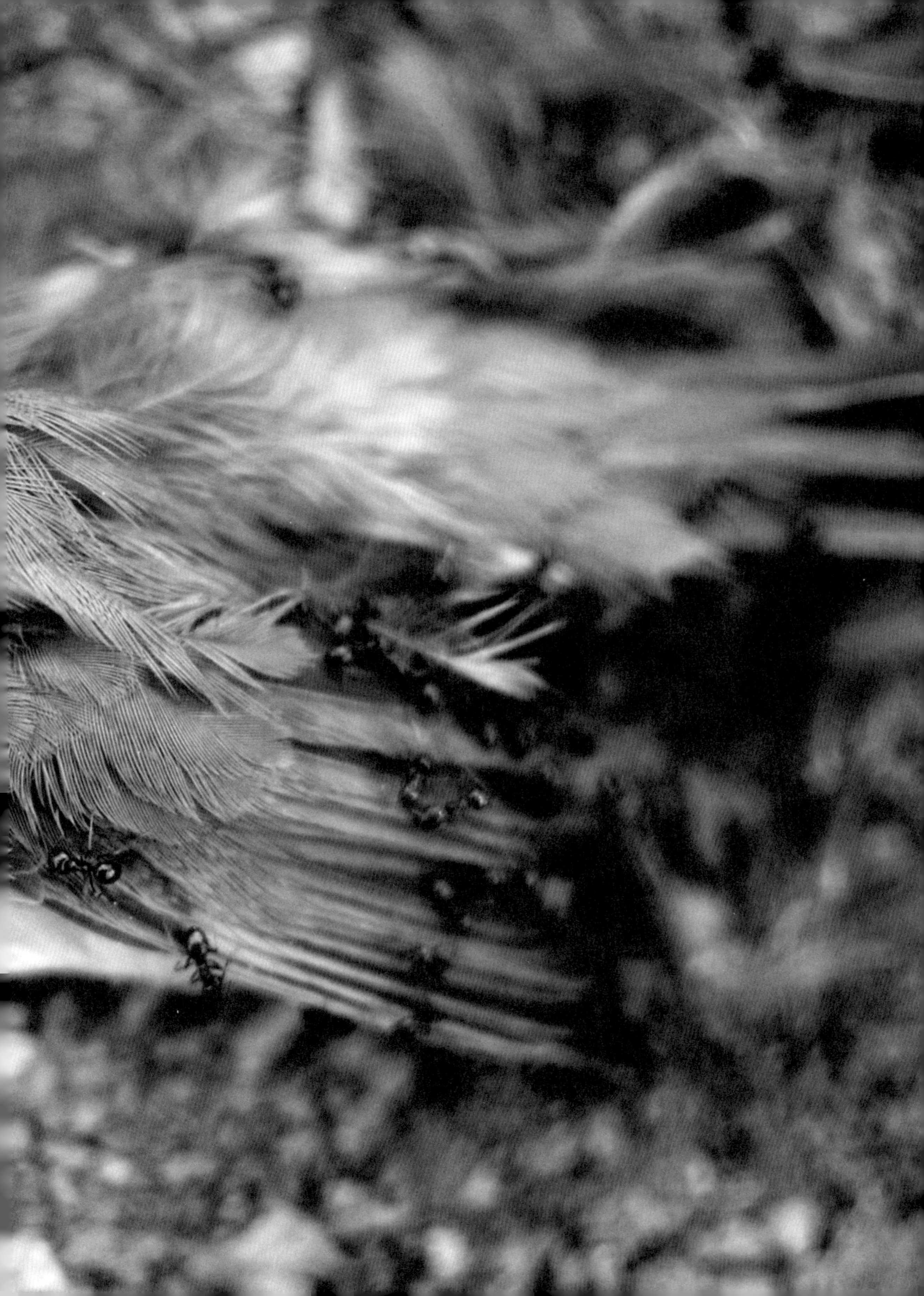

They explain to me that
I have to make myself
available, that I have
to make it easy for men
to do what they want
with me. If I'm "good,"
there will be money.
How much am I worth?
Toys, candies, or special
care are my rewards.
If I resist, I will be
punished.

A delivery vehicle is transporting children.
No one speaks a word
during the drive, every-
one keeps their eyes
fixed to the floor. Then
we enter a darkened
building. My arms are
bound over my head.
I see a naked girl stand-
ing next to me.

Two men wearing
hoods stick something
between her legs and
squeeze her neck, choke
her. I am forced to go
fetch other children
and to bring them to
the middle of a room
for the Black Mass.
Many scenes happen
simultaneously,
ritual practices are
performed. Infants
are tortured.

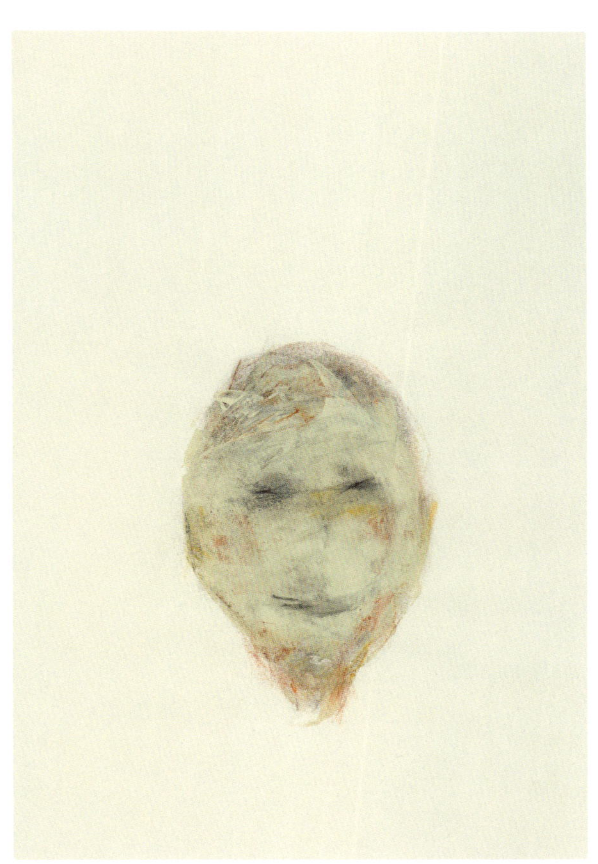

One is on the floor, strapped by the wrists and ankles in the form of an X, and surrounded by a ring of candles. Someone begins to cut the child. Another one, whose gaze rests upon me, bears severe wounds on the head and upper body.

My body feels like it's crippled, paralyzed. I hardly have enough strength to remain standing. I'm short of breath and feel like I'm sinking into a deep hole.

I was conditioned and manipulated to perform certain roles in these pedophile circles. What have I done?

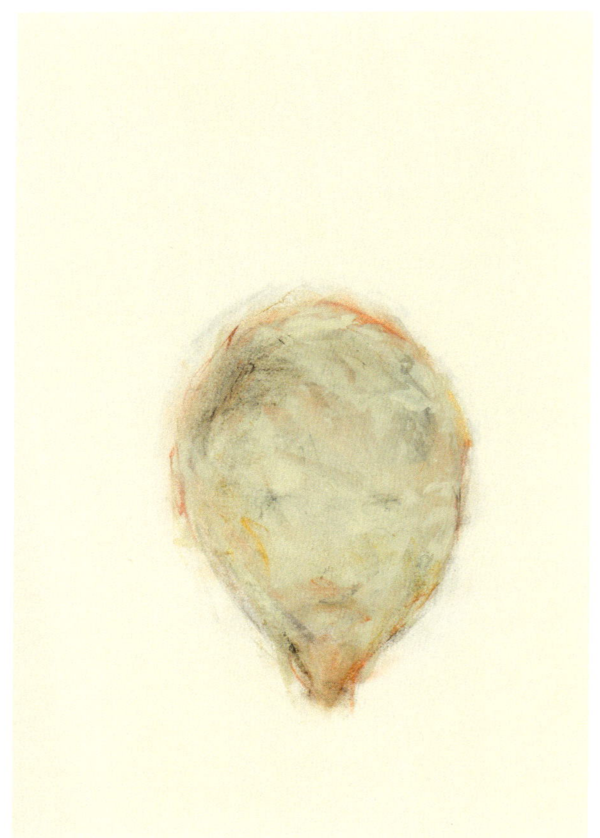

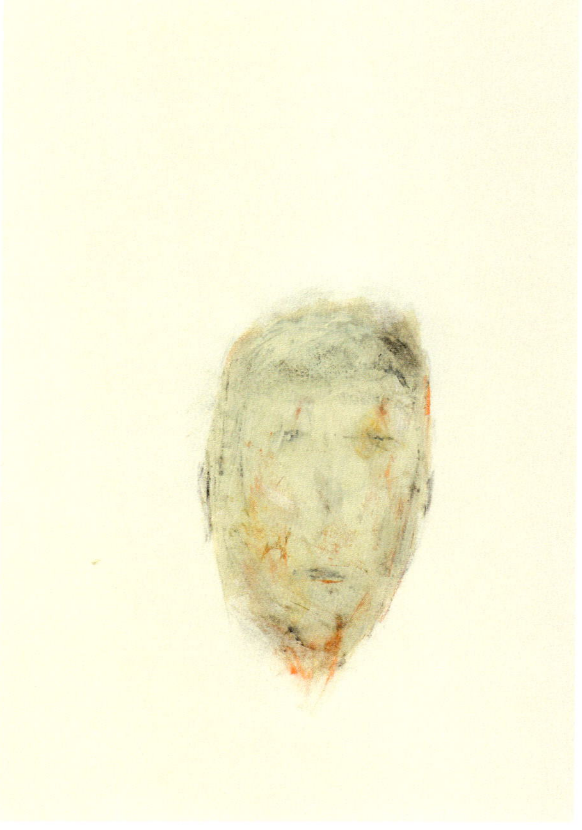

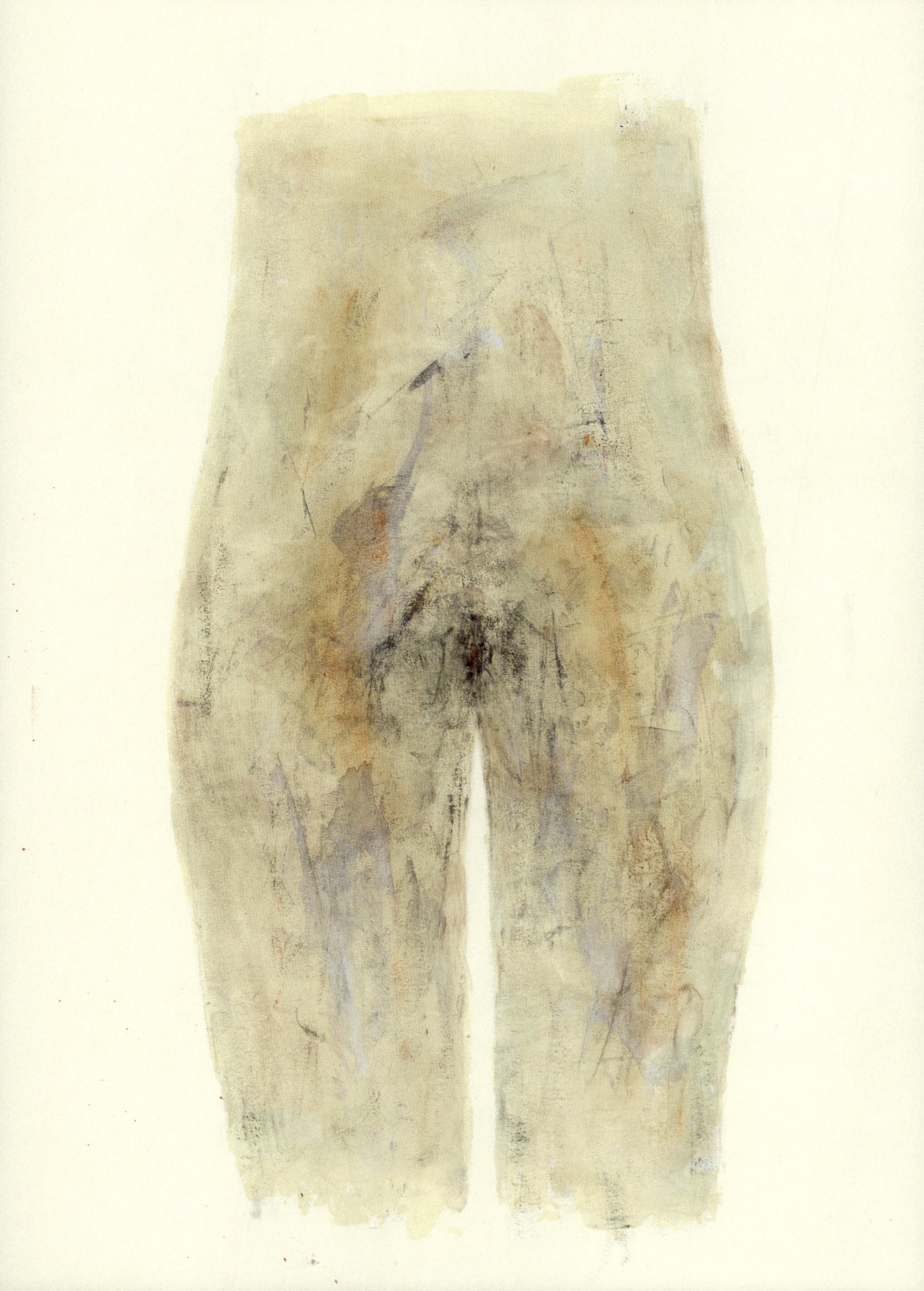

I am free of guilt.

After many days of stupor, I have started to **regain a little bit of confidence.** At some point it must suffice to have confronted the things that I dread. It's a process of healing from all that horror. The people who have mistreated me are insignificant and fearful. They backed off when faced with the strength and determination that have protected me from resignation, from giving up.

My special history and the pain I was **made to inflict upon others are a heavy burden.** The feelings of shame and loneliness are still with me today. I was not alone in my suffering and yet I alone shoulder the guilt for having carried out the orders and causing so much pain.

I dream of butterflies who visit me, take the weight from my soul, and tell me that I am free of guilt.

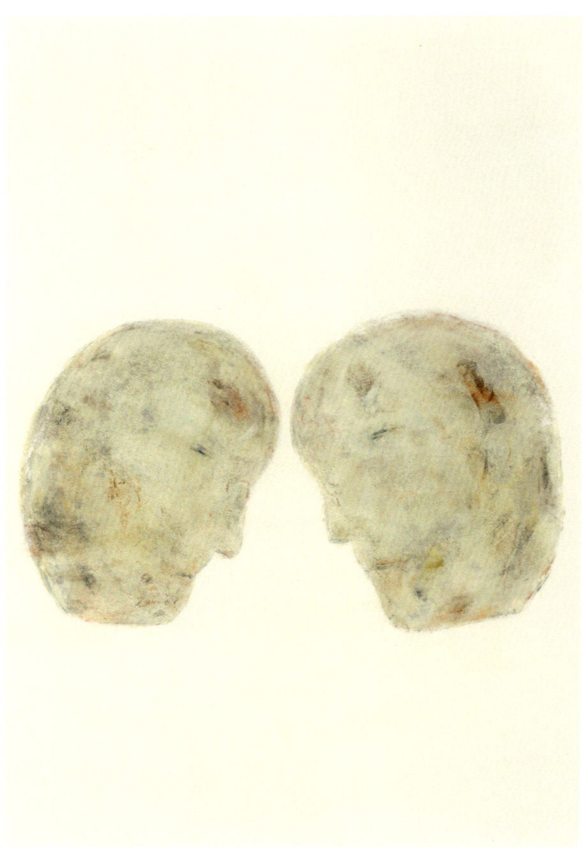

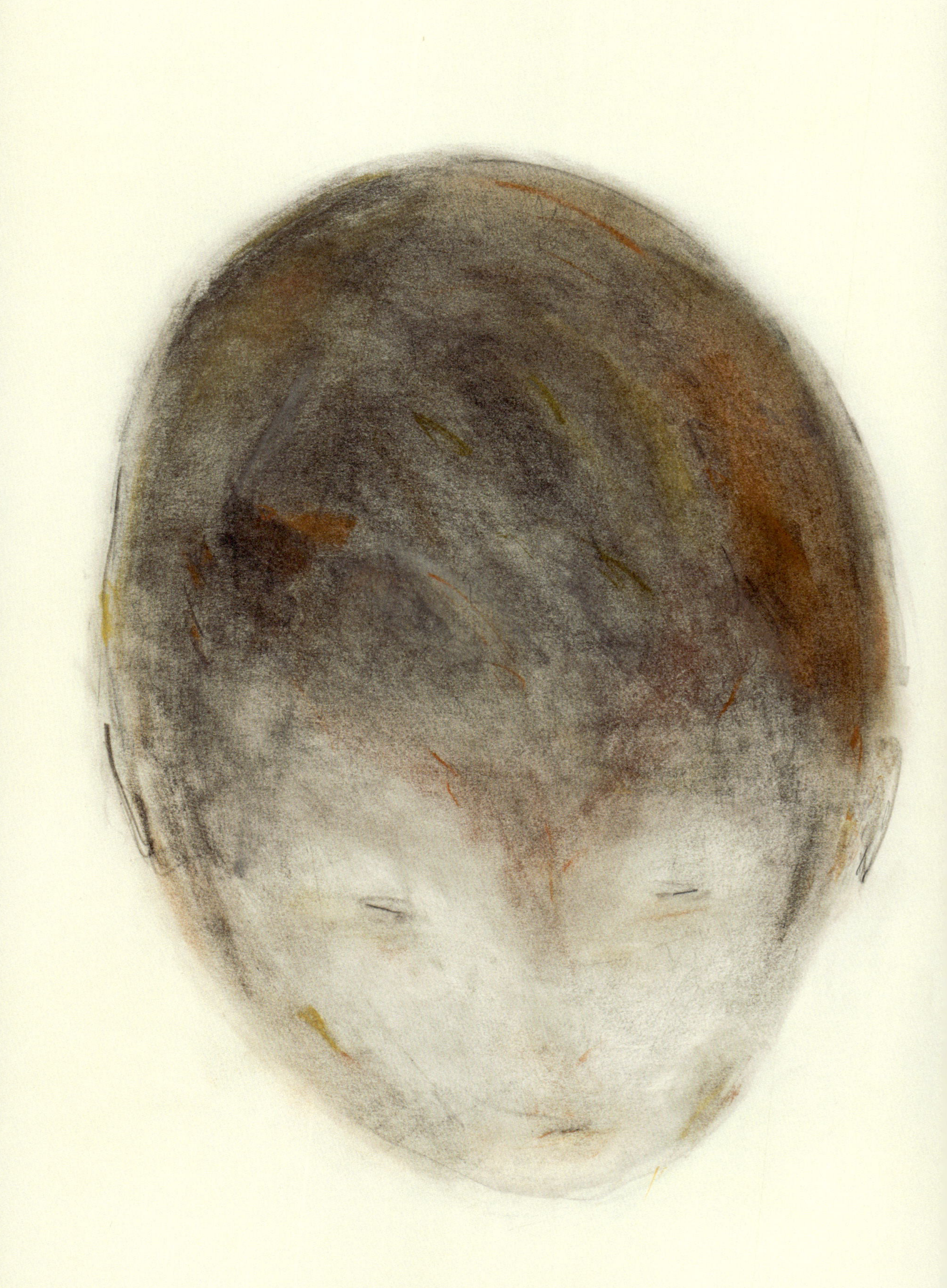

**The path no longer leads into obscurity
but rather into the light.**

I paint fantastic dream landscapes
of the type that saved me as a child
from being destroyed by my experiences.
There is so much power
in the world of the imagination.

I step out of the long shadows
for now and forever
and move forward in my own fullness
as a radiant being.

Love, protection, and security

*
CRC **Preamble**
"Recognizing that the child, for the full and harmonious development of his or her personality, should grow up in a family environment, in an atmosphere of happiness, love and understanding."

Article 19, Paragraph 1
"States Parties shall take all appropriate legislative, administrative, social and educational means to protect the child from all forms of physical or mental violence, injury or abuse, neglect or negligent treatment, maltreatment or exploitation, including sexual abuse, while in the care of parent(s), legal guardian(s) or any other person who has the care of the child."

Article 3, Paragraph 2
The State Party is under the obligation "to ensure the child such protection and care as is necessary for his or her well-being," and **Article 20** to "ensure alternative care" to "a child temporarily or permanently deprived of his or her family environment." There are different ways to guarantee the rights of these children, preferably in family-like care arrangements, which must be carefully examined with respect to the risk of these children being exposed to violence.

This book is appearing at a time
when the international community
is observing the thirtieth anniversary
of the United Nations Convention
on the Rights of the Child (CRC)*
and when I, myself, am completing work
on a global study on children
deprived of liberty.

This will be the third global study
to focus on children,
following the 1996 report by Graça Machel
on the *Impact of armed conflict on children*
and the 2006 *World report on violence
against children* by Paulo Sérgio Pinheiro.
These reports deal ultimately
with the issue of violence:
the brutal recruitment of child combatants
who are forced to commit unthinkable acts
of violence, mainly against civilians,
including other children;
corporal punishment and other forms
of physical, mental, and sexual violence
against children — in the family,
at school, in children's homes,
at boarding schools, or other institutions
in which children are kept largely
against their will; violence in prisons,
police stations, and migration-related detention;
and ritual abuse of the type
Laurent Ziegler so powerfully describes.

Laurent Ziegler recalls
how he was coerced as a child
to actively participate in ritual violence,
much as armed extremist or terrorist groups
such as the Islamic State
force child soldiers to kill or maim other people.
Child soldiers can remain traumatized
and plagued by feelings of guilt,
and Laurent Ziegler has likewise
experienced guilt for acts
he was forced to commit as a child.
This book represents his effort
to address these guilty feelings
in an extremely courageous, honest,
and unflinching way.

In the aforementioned UN global study,
on the basis of widely comprehensive data
collected for this purpose,
I came to the conclusion that there are
more than seven million children worldwide
who are currently "deprived of liberty."
The majority are in specialized care institutions
for "difficult children," children with disabilities,
or children who have been orphaned,
abandoned, or separated for other reasons
from their parents.

I spoke with many of these children,
and they confirmed that violence
is part of their daily experience.
What they felt they lacked in their lives
was love, protection, and security,
and it is the longing for these qualities —
love, protection, and security — that is
also a recurring theme throughout
Laurent Ziegler's *The childhood of my memory.*

My work on the global study
served as a terrifying reminder
of the extreme cruelty
that adults are capable of inflicting
on the young and of the effect
that such physical, mental, verbal,
and sexual violence can have on children.
One of the most important goals
of the Convention on the Rights of the Child,
which has been ratified by nearly
all of the world's countries,
is to ensure that children enjoy a childhood
free from fear and violence
and that the child should be enabled
to grow up in an atmosphere of love,
protection, and security,
ideally in a family
or "family-like care" environment.

I hope that, with this impressive
and courageous book, Laurent Ziegler
will find the help he needs
to recover from his own violent upbringing
and that other children will be spared
the experience of such a childhood.
However, this will only be possible
if adults finally accept that every form
of violence against children
is prohibited by law and that they
can be prosecuted if they engage in it.

Manfred Nowak

Manfred Nowak
is Professor of International Human Rights at the University of Vienna, Founder and long-standing Co-director of the Ludwig Boltzmann Institute for Human Rights (until April 2019), General Secretary of the Global Campus of Human Rights in Venice, Italy (since 2016) and Director of the Vienna Master of Arts in Applied Human Rights at the University of Applied Arts in Vienna, Austria (since 2020). In addition, he has served, among other things, as United Nations Special Rapporteur on Torture (2004–2010) and Independent Expert leading the United Nations Global Study on Children Deprived of Liberty (2016–2019).

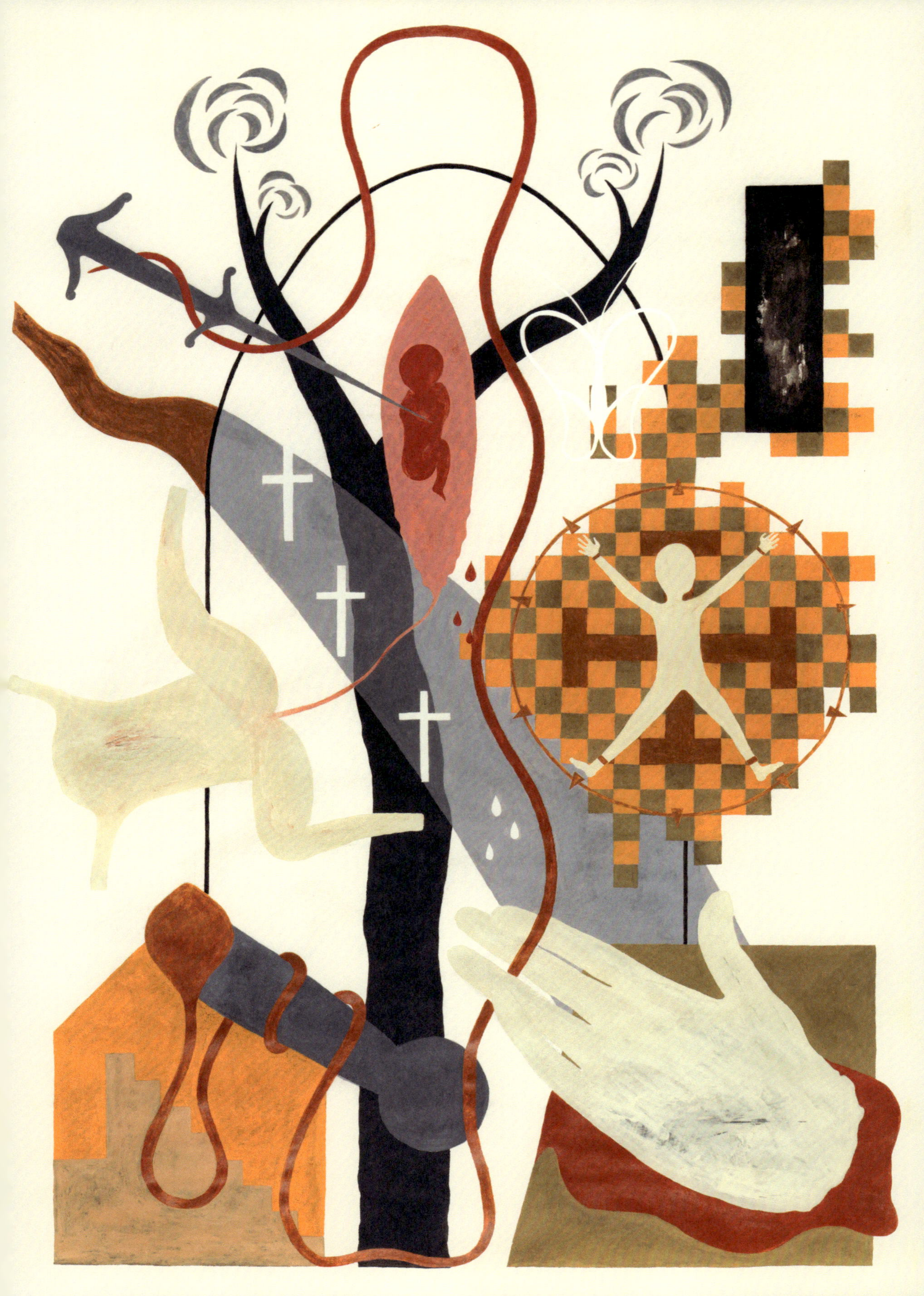

Almost everything
is too much.

Dear Laurent, we have known each other
for a good number of years — 15 to be exact.
I'm grateful for your continued existence
in this world, a reality often not assured.
Children who must navigate
the sinister realms of pedophile rings
cannot emerge unscathed.
Some succumb and die, others are
institutionalized with dissociative disorders,
some seek solace in substances,
while others resort to selling their bodies
or become perpetrators themselves,
trying to gain power in the same circles
that abused them.
Some wander aimlessly,
their lives devoid of meaning,
reduced to mere survival.

Laurent, when you asked me to speak
at the opening of your exhibit,
my answer was a resounding "yes."
Yet, when sitting at home
alone with your book,
I found myself asking,
what should I say?

I've witnessed your journey —
the stages of fear, shock, despair, horror,
shame, guilt, anger, and grief
through which you have passed.
I've lived through them with you
time and time again, but to see them
vividly depicted in your book
left me breathless.
The sheer terror overwhelmed and numbed me.
How do we find words for the unspeakable?
This is precisely what makes your book
and art so extraordinary.
It is the endeavor of a remarkable artist
to wrestle words from horror,
to render it in images, making it tangible.

The question is not,
"Do such things really happen?"
or "How can people do this to others?"
We know such atrocities occur.
The ongoing Bergisch-Gladbach trials
in Germany provide a glimpse
into the sickening abuse
and torture captured on video
that are almost impossible to watch,
as even the police officers
whose duty it was to review the videos
have reported.

Books, films,
research papers, and news articles
attempt to address these issues.
Perhaps our minds
can begin to comprehend
the words we hear and read
about the abuse of children,
child pornography, and child trafficking.
However, only those scarred by violence
can truly understand
the profound impact of growing up
under such conditions.
The real question is not "Can this happen?"
but "How can a child survive
and, beyond survival, embrace life?"

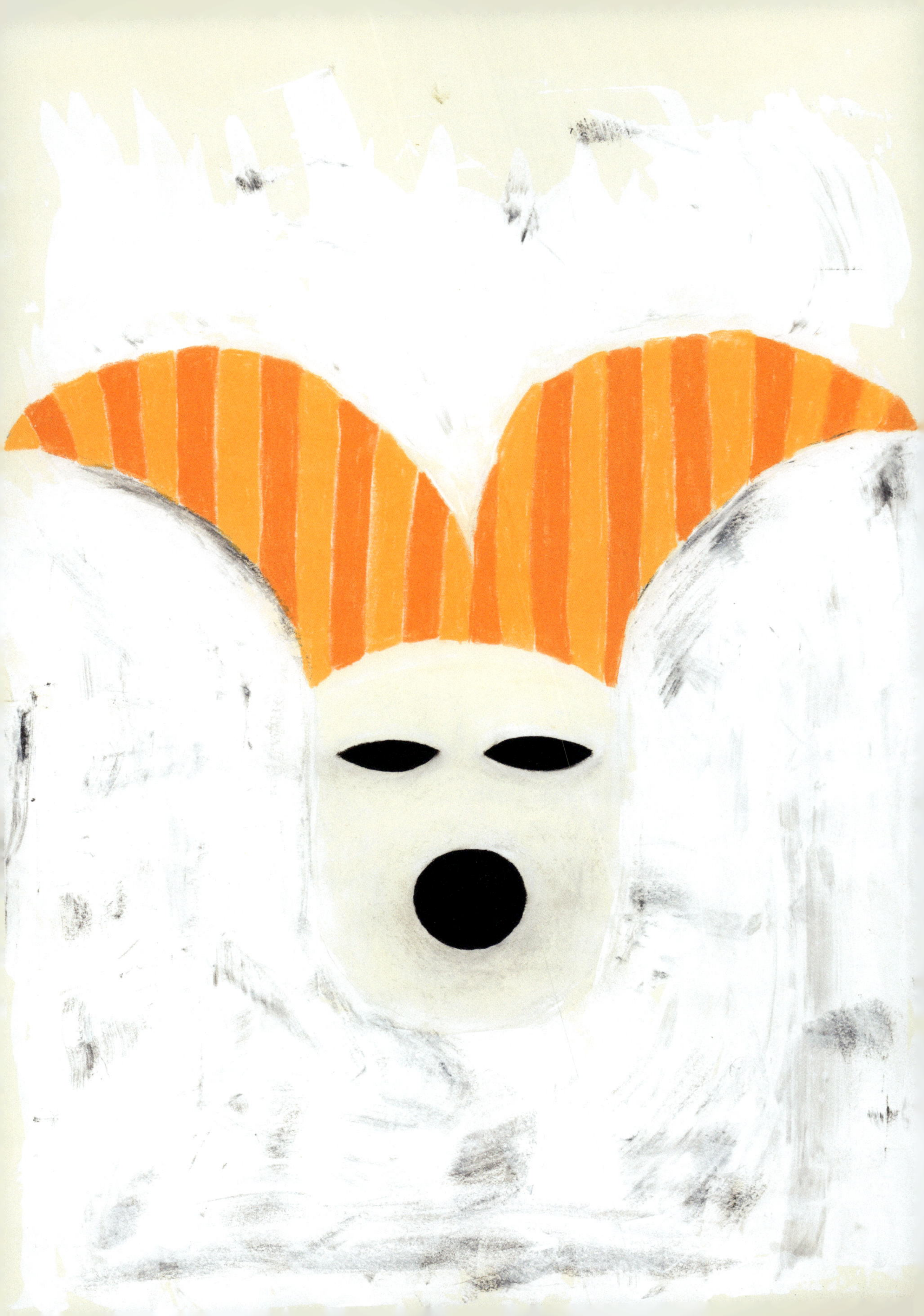

Children subjected to brutality
instead of love struggle
to differentiate between perpetrator
and victim.
The conclusion they draw is
that there is no such thing
as safety in this world.
Whatever horrors they endure
are their own fault
because they are not worthy of love.

The ensuing shame can lead
to the development of coping mechanisms
such as the adoption of roles and masks,
twisting and contorting themselves
to conform with societal expectations
while obeying the taboo of silence,
to ensure that their true selves remain hidden,
even if this means living a life in complete
isolation.

Laurent, in crafting this book,
embodies the utmost courage — the courage
to discard masks and to reveal oneself,
naked, in moments of fear,
guilt, and shame.

The greatest gift
we human beings can offer each other
is to listen without judgment.
That's what we're called upon to do today —
to be still, quietly attentive,
to open our hearts, to engage with Laurent
as he unveils his world, inviting us to see,
hear, smell, taste, and feel.
For that is exactly what his art achieves;
it engages all of our senses.

If this seems overwhelming,
if the words and images are "too much,"
acknowledge the feelings
of someone who has managed to survive.
Let it in, for this is the emotional burden
that survivors must carry in this world,
without ever being able
to lay it down.

In modern life, for trauma survivors
almost everything can seem too much—
the demands that society places on us,
at school, at work, and in our
interpersonal or other relationships.
Other people can be intimidating.
They may trigger the instinct to escape,
to hide or run away, to diminish ourselves
into invisibility.
As a result, there is an urgency
to do something, anything, quickly
before the anxiety returns,
bringing with it the sleeplessness,
unbearable pain, stress, and tension,
and other dreadful emotions
so strong that it makes it hard to breathe.
Manifesting in panic attacks,
feelings of emptiness, futility, depression,
and even self-harm, these emotions
leave one without a reliable compass
to navigate a seemingly alien world.
The outside world
filled with laughter and joy
is only visible through a dim window,
offering no hope and no entry point.
It is this overwhelming sense of "too much"
that can ultimately
lead to a complete breakdown,
halting life in its tracks
with screeching finality.

This inner process involves
navigating the threshold between life and death.
It becomes paramount in one's healing
and self-awareness to discern
between two distinct states of consciousness…
The one being:
"I can't stand this pain any longer.
It's all too much!
I don't want to be in this world anymore.
I want to die."
The other asking the question:
"Who or what wants to die?
Is it me or some facets of me?
I want these emotions to go away.
I want those aspects of myself
that are ensnared in the horror,
reliving physical trauma, and drowning
in feelings of isolation and futility,
to die and find peace in their demise."

No one can avoid an eventual confrontation
with the inevitability of death.
In fact, for human beings, nothing instills
more fear than the fear of death.
It is this unconscious fear that pursues
us through life, unleashing incredible powers.
Confronting and surmounting
this fear enables us to evolve
into lives of self-responsibility
and empowerment.
The life force, once liberated,
can manifest itself not as fear
but as a path for creation.
The perpetual, forceful "doing"
may then yield
to a serene state of being.

By allowing ourselves
to confront and conquer
our personal demons,
as Laurent has done,
we can rediscover
life with such intensity
that it can resemble
a state of rebirth.

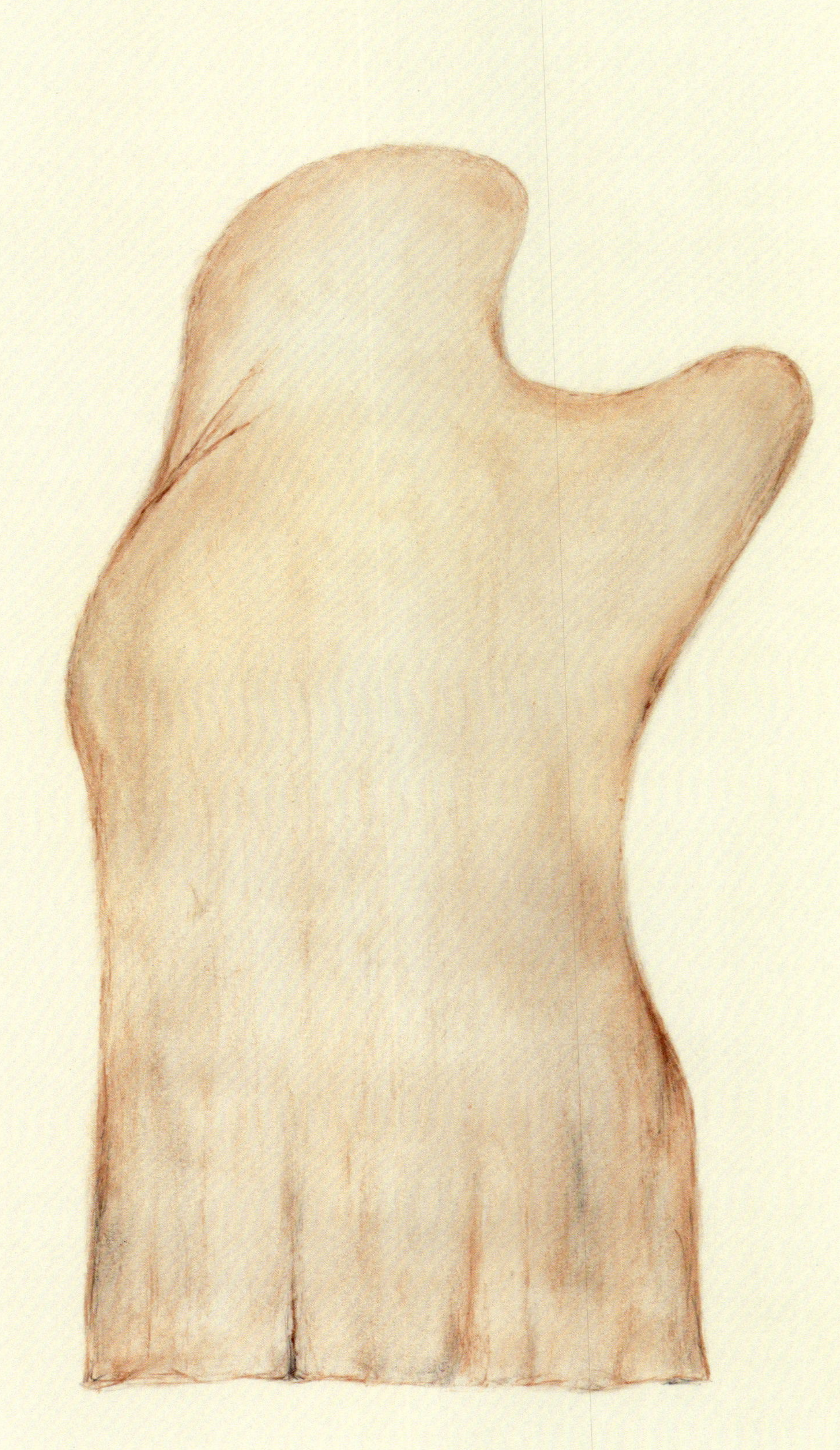

Laurent's paintings and writings
make all of this tangible
and reveal the incredible beauty
of the human soul
intertwining the beautiful
and the ugly,
the good and the bad,
the light and the dark.
Human capacity
lies in embracing this duality,
experiencing it as a whole.
As Carl Gustav Jung once wrote:
"Those who can perceive
their shadow and light simultaneously
can see themselves from two sides
and can thus arrive in their center."

Dear Laurent,
your book exemplifies this journey.
Your will, echoing Viktor Frankl's
"say yes to life, in spite of everything,"
allowed you to confront inner demons.
You transformed fear into trust,
guilt into sensitivity,
shame into self-empowerment,
and embraced compassion
not only for yourself
but for all beings,
even the perpetrators.
It is this love that enables a deeper connection
to oneself, others, the greater whole,
and the essence of being human
and alive.

I thank you for this gift,
hoping the world will benefit,
serving as a testament to your inner triumph
and shedding light on the "wonder of life."
This miracle we all may experience
if we look inside. I invite everyone
to use this moment to do exactly that,
to lower the barriers
and celebrate this wonderful,
exuberant, crazy world,
with all that it encompasses,
its darkness and light.

Sonja Busch

Introductory words
on the occasion of
the exhibition opening
by Laurent Ziegler,
"The childhood of my
memory — Painting,
Drawing, Photography,"
at the Gallery Jünger
in Vienna on September 16, 2020.

Sonja Busch
After studying political science, sociology, and education in Frankfurt am Main and gaining initial professional experience in New York, Hamburg, and Berlin, Sonja began working for the OSCE Organization for Security and Co-operation in Europe as Democratization Officer in Bosnia and Herzegovina in the late 1990s. From 2003 to 2007, she held responsibilities for various international organizations and large multilateral projects combating human trafficking. In 2007, she established herself as an independent consultant and clinical supervisor for organizations and teams concentrating on gender-based violence and trauma. Since 2014, her focus has increasingly shifted to the therapeutic field.

She now works in her private practice with an emphasis on Transpersonal Psychology and body therapy in Vienna. In addition, she coordinates the GTT European Grof Training Program in Transpersonal Psychology and Holotropic Breathwork and is founder of the European Association of Holotropic Breathwork.

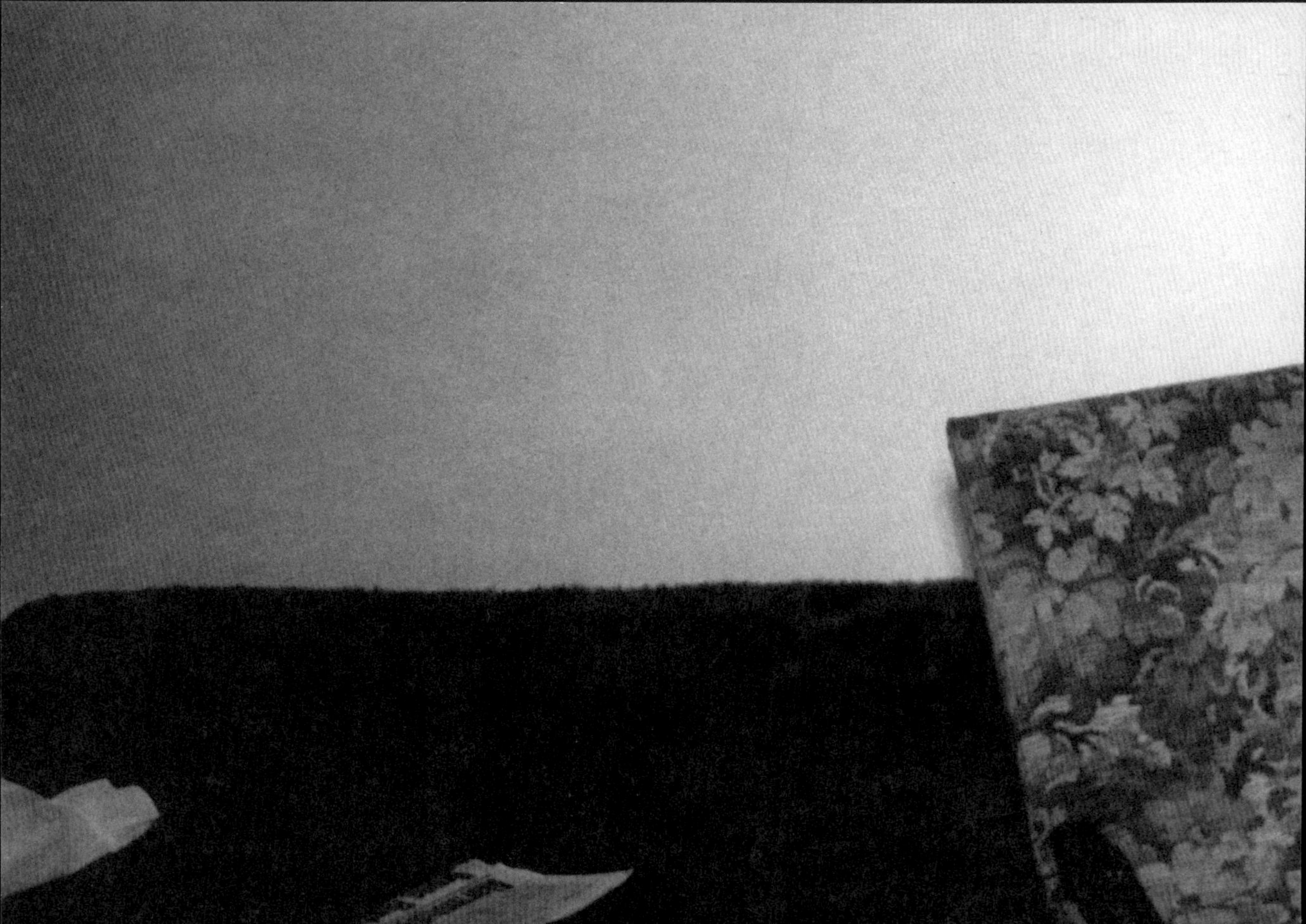

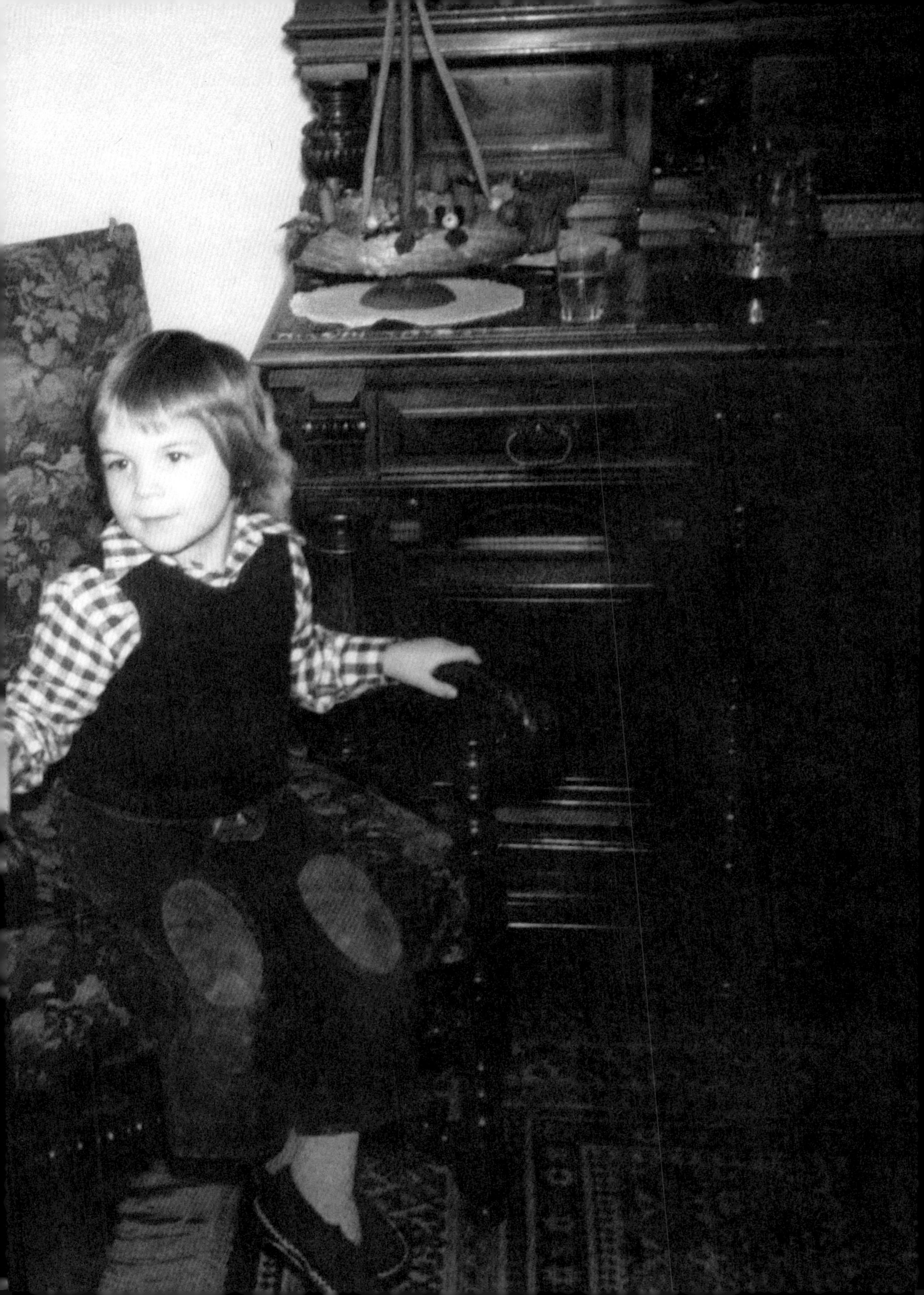

**My legs, my feet
are re-learning how to carry me.
I regain trust in them,**
how they anchor me to the earth,
much like a tree.
I feel the soft footprints,
warmth begins to rise
and to thaw my body out of its paralysis.

**Everything good grows towards me
as my heart begins to glow.**
I am grateful for today's experiences
and for this abundance of life.

One day, I could no longer return.
A door closed,
but a part of my inner self
remained with the other children.
Will this portal ever open again?

**Back then, something died,
ceased to live.**
As a result of punishment or a ritual,
my neck stiffens and I freeze.
Stifled for air, I embark on a "journey,"
my heart captured in deepest dreams.

I continue to beat and to punish myself.
My body is my escort, armor, and shield;
an object, externalized,
limitless, procurable, and for sale.
My body never belonged to me.

**I paint myself underneath the earth,
in a coffin, a grave, cut off,
covered over with soil, in darkness, forgotten.**
I am anxious
to open my arms and to ascend
into the blue sky.

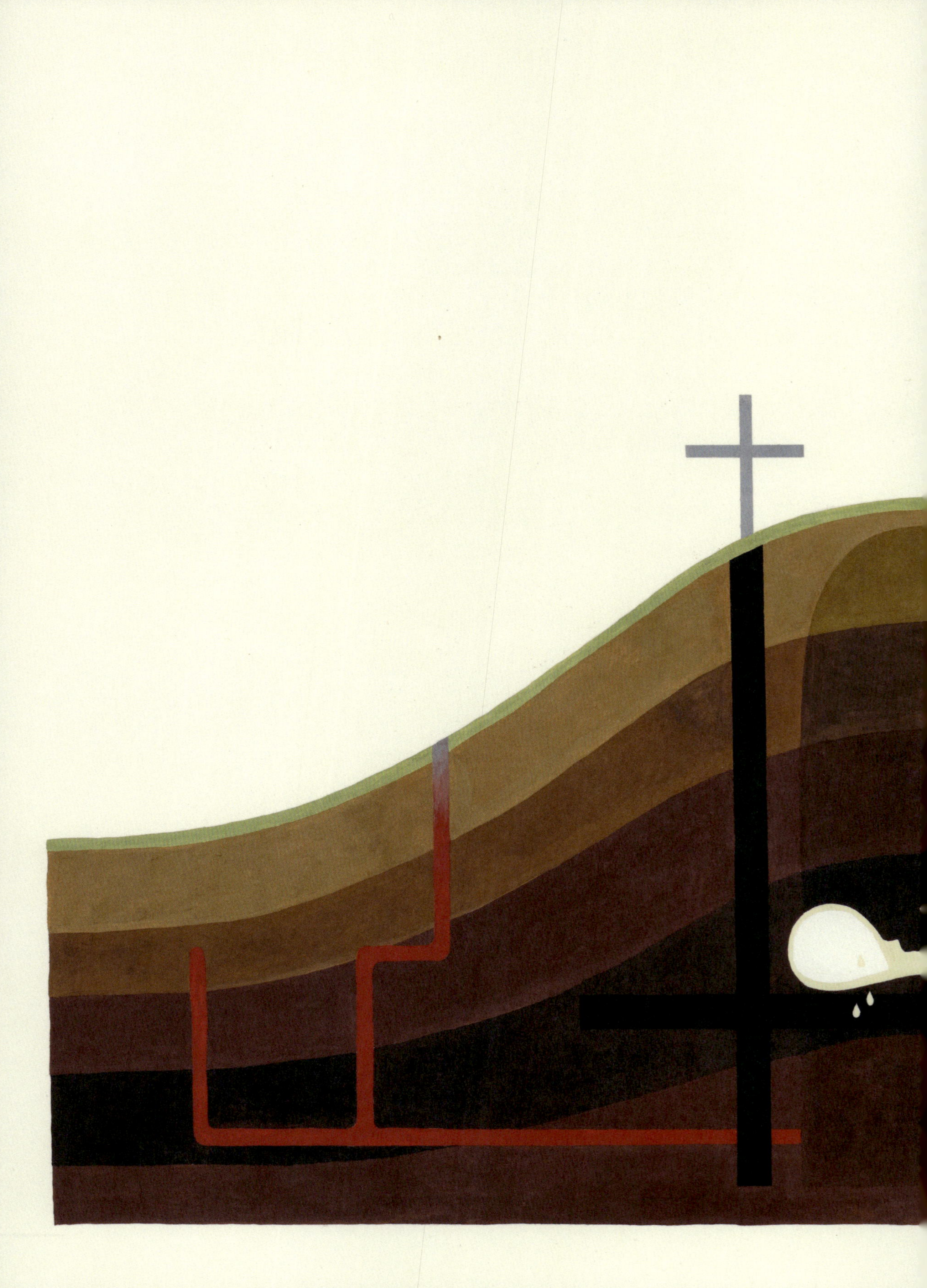

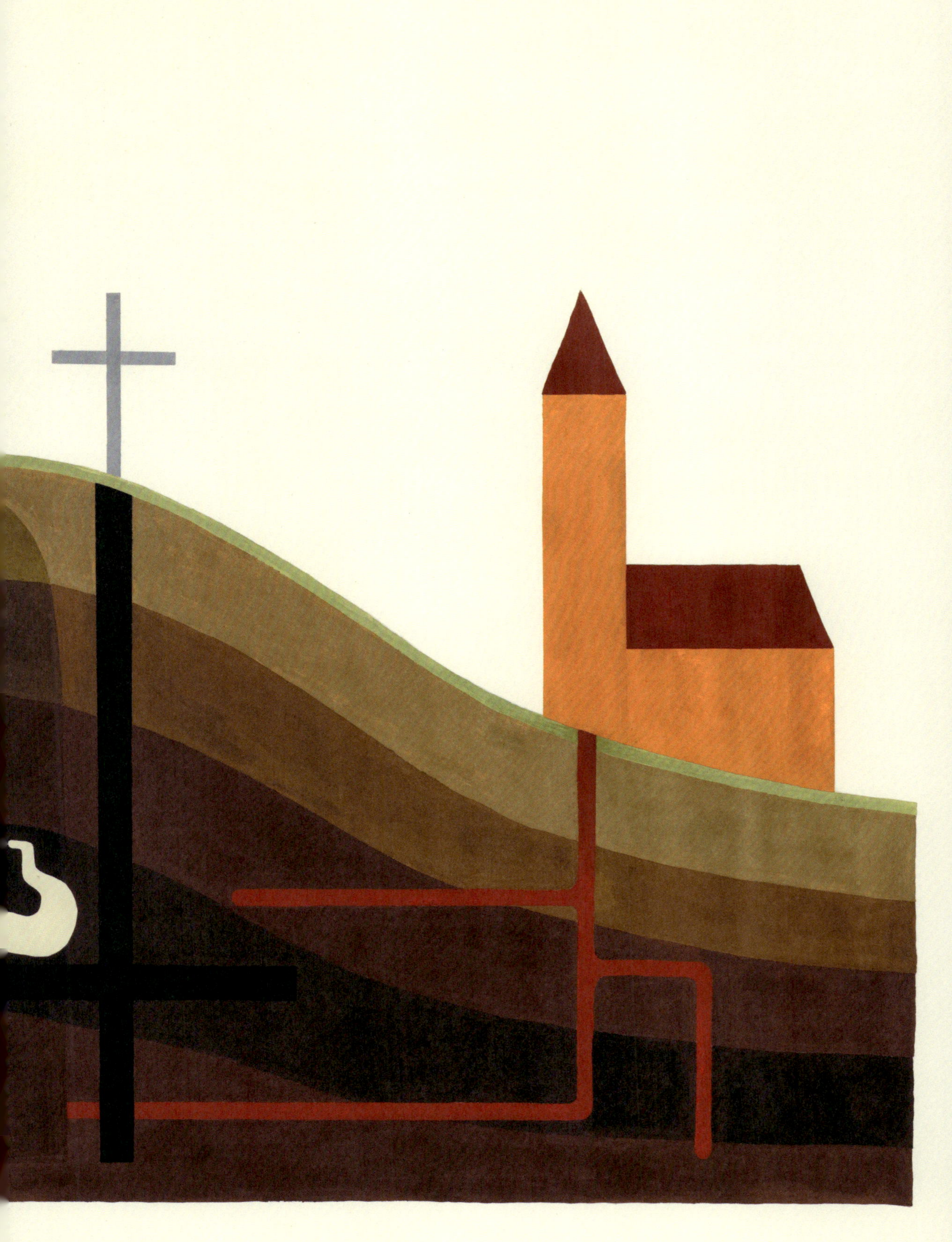

How often have I left
my body and gone
"traveling"? There is
the rolling, compressing
moaning of lifeless
children. Their skin is
so white. Am I dead
and seeing myself
from above?

They grab us by
the collars and push
us down channels
like animals. The pain
is still there in my
neck, hands, and feet.
Scattered fragments
of my body are
coming back together,
gradually and with
difficulty.

I have to decide the
fate of other lives.
I am not present within
or outside of myself.
Some are caught up in
a frenzy of power and
blood. I sense the breath,
the stroking of other
children.

They are buried.
I am them, see myself
in their eyes, die with
them, am one with
them. I run away.

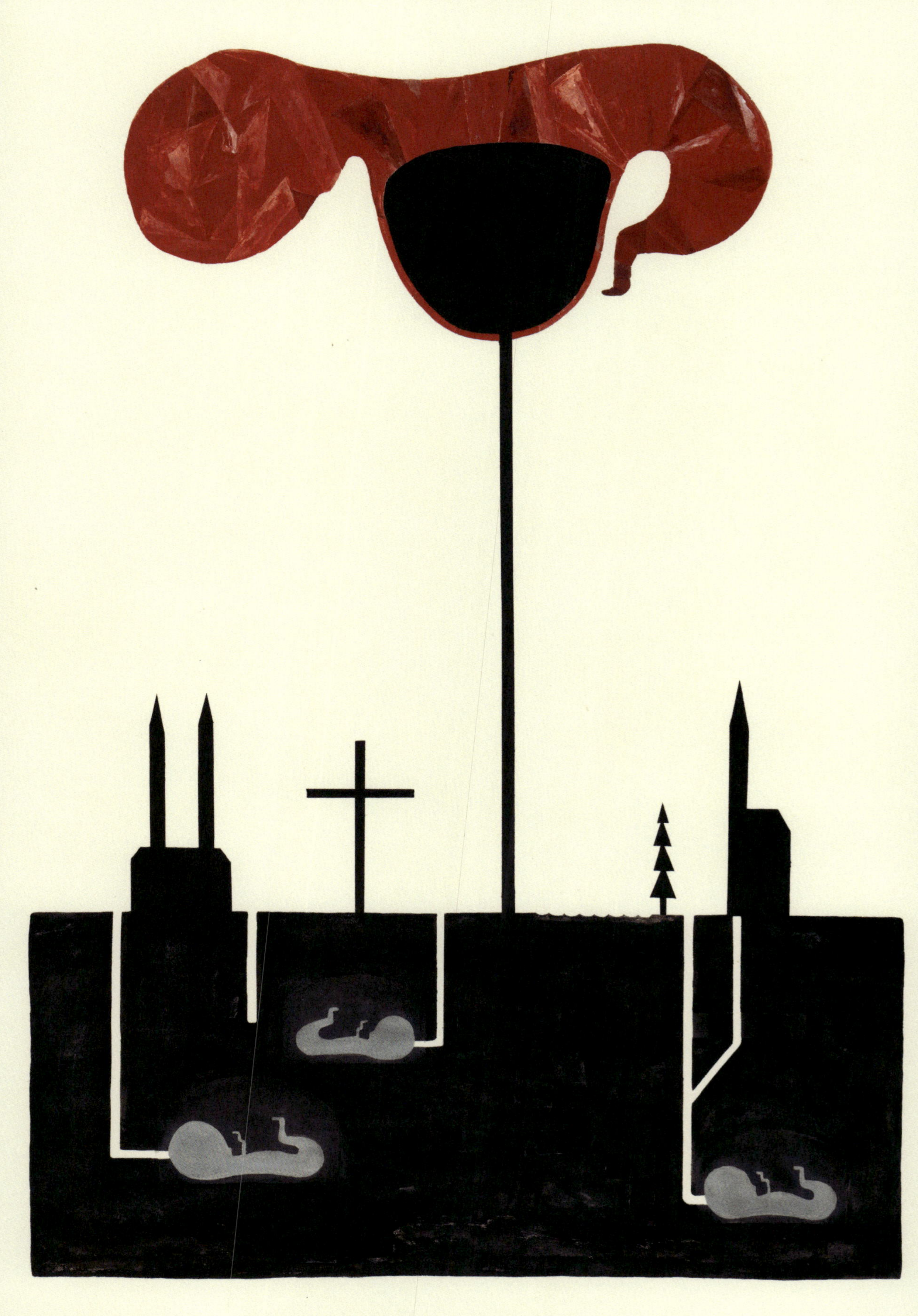

I am alone.
The child in me calls me to come home.

Scars heal.

In every embrace, I feel forgiveness
and yet freeze before finding
a way to be.

With the passage of time,
intimacy gives way to a place
so empty and full of longing.

I quietly draw a circle,
fall into a night alienated from dreams,
and conceal my world.

I am free, my soul is free,
my heart is free.

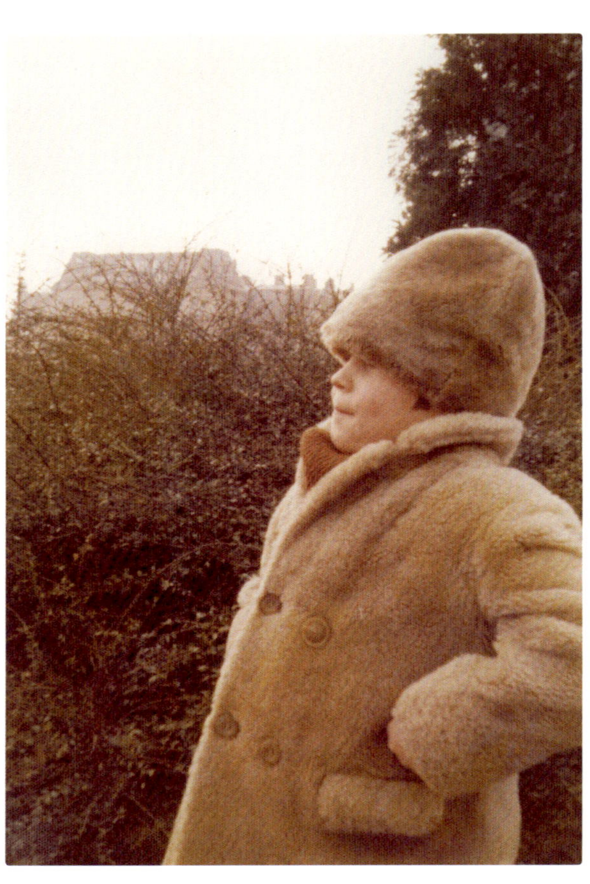

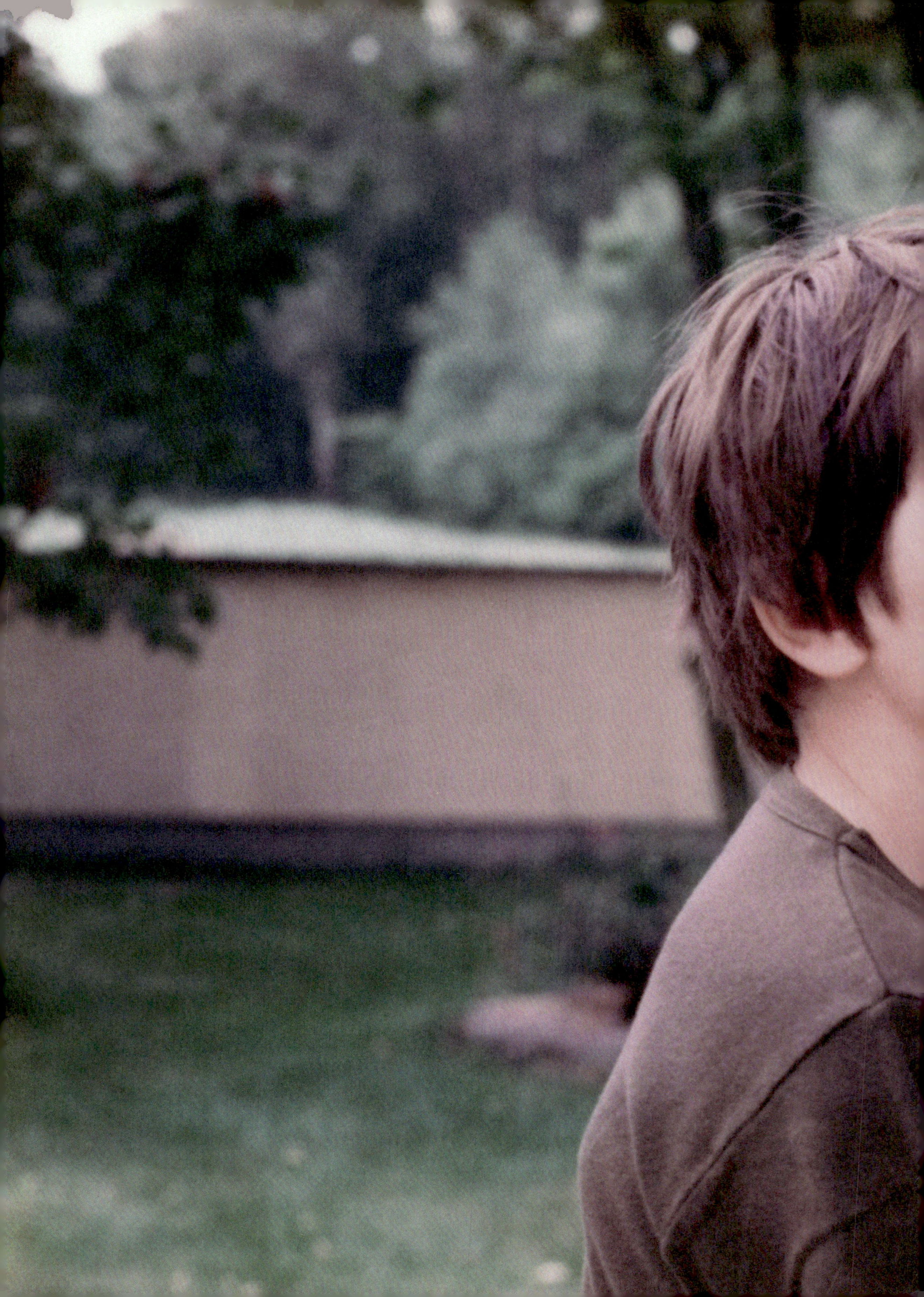

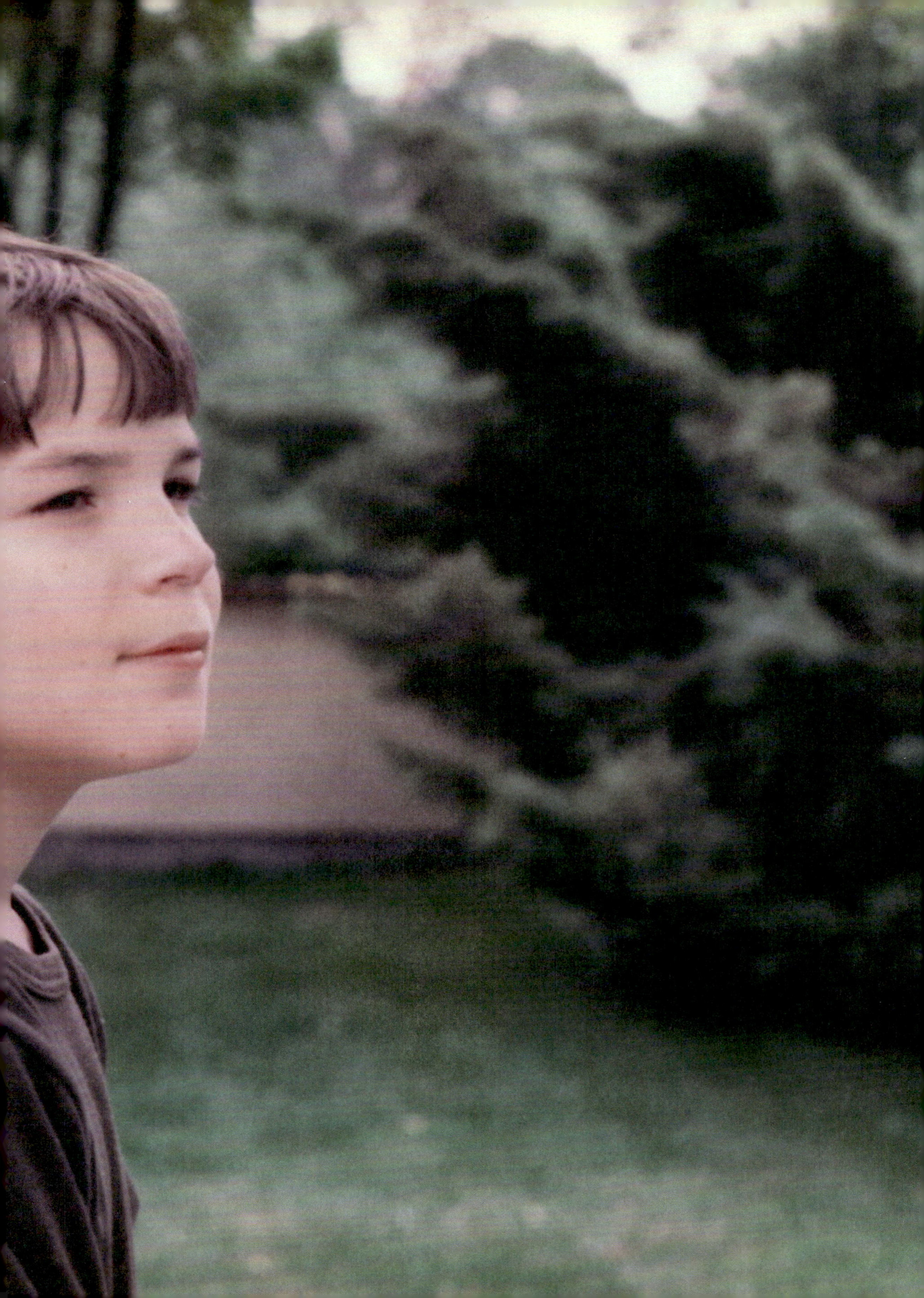

Published by
VfmK Verlag für moderne Kunst GmbH
Schwedenplatz 2/24 | 1010 Vienna | Austria | hello@vfmk.org | www.vfmk.org

ISBN 978-3-99153-158-6

All rights reserved
2025 © Laurent Ziegler, the authors, the artists, the photographers,
Verlag für moderne Kunst, Vienna | Printed in Austria

Distribution
- Europe: LKG | www.lkg.eu
- USA and worldwide: D.A.P. | www.artbook.com

Bibliographic information published by the Deutsche Nationalbibliothek
The Deutsche Nationalbibliothek lists this publication in the Deutsche Nationalbibliografie;
detailed bibliographic data are available on the Internet at www.dnb.de

Text Page 01
»Extraio meus sentimentos e palavras da minha noite absoluta.«
Clarice Lispector from *Um Sopro de Vida*, 1978

Editor
Laurent Ziegler

Concept
Laurent Ziegler and Clemens Theobert Schedler

Paintings, drawings, texts and photographs
Laurent Ziegler, except pages 16 | 17 und 84 | 85 Raki Nikahetiya | *www.rakiography.com*
and pages 2 | 3, 9, 114, 125 und 126 | 127 Private property

Essays
Sonja Busch and Manfred Nowak

Translations
KeK

Copyediting and proofreading
Brian Dorsey and Claudia Mazanek

Image editing and pre-press
Markus Wörgötter

Book design
Clemens Theobert Schedler, Büro für konkrete Gestaltung

Typeface
Korpus, designed by Mika Mischler und Nik Thönen | *www.binnenland.ch*

Papers
- ECOREL PRESTO SI ECP14576 ivory, 150 gr
- SURBALIN plain 6082 violett, 115 gr
- SALZER Design White, bulk 1.5, 150 gr

Printing
Holzhausen, the book brand of Gerin Druck GmbH
TEAM Johannes Fauland, Klara Gogoljak and Beate Koller

Binding
Buchbinderei Papyrus GesmbH & Co KG

First edition
500 Copies in January 2025

**The publication was made possible
through the generous support of**

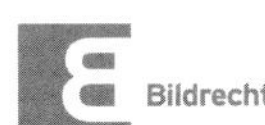

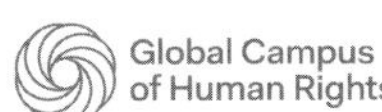

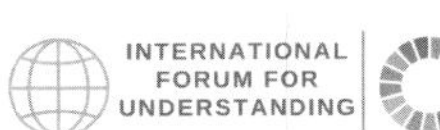

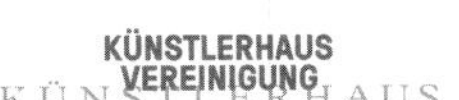

Acknowledgements
- Andrès Gonzales
- Anna Pultar
- Avi Septimus
- Barbara Sidoti
- Bettina Hofbauer
- Bo Madsen
- Brian Carolan
- Brigitte Heidinger
- Caroline Sander
- Cathrine Stukhard
- Christian Bazant-Hegemark
- Christine Slavik
- Daniel Winklehner
- Elizabeth Maclean
- Esther Hladik | born Mlenek
- Eva-Maria Maurer
- Finn Landsteiner
- Gerlinde Riegler
- Günther Huber
- Heather Wokusch
- Helmut Prochart
- Helmut Sax
- Ian Digges
- Jelena Kopanja
- Johannes and Silvia Kaup
- Julian Fink
- Karen Janssen
- Karl Fink
- Karolina Milewicz
- Kendall Alaimo
- Lothar and Sabine Trierenberg
- Mădălina Bot
- Maja Petrovic
- Marco Araujo
- Mariana Schönauer
- Marlene Heinrich
- Michael Rapp
- Monika Froehler
- Nataliya Kudelya
- Nebahat Gueney
- Nensi Veljanovski
- Nikolaus Selimov
- Orsolya Toth Toth
- Peter Hohenhaus
- Raki Nikahetiya
- Romulus Varga
- Sabine Bockting
- Sally McMullen
- Sandra Zečević Penić
- Silke Albert
- Stephan Darwall
- Szilard Robert Halasz
- Tanja Cochlar
- Theresa Kamelander
- Ordination5
- Thomas Liska
- Ute Langthaler
- Veronika Floch
- Veronika Rajmanova
- Zuzana Saganova